# The Genius of Justice

2/18/23

Dear Roy,

Thank you for being a genius of justice. Your biblical & theological work inspires me each day! May God continue to bless & keep you witnessing & working for justice.

Love, faith & friendship,

Jim Ahern

# The **Genius** of **Justice**

Timothy C. Ahrens

FOREWORD BY
Walter Brueggemann

CASCADE *Books* · Eugene, Oregon

THE GENIUS OF JUSTICE

Cascade Books
An Imprint of Wipf and Stock Publishers
199 W. 8th Ave., Suite 3
Eugene, OR 97401

www.wipfandstock.com

PAPERBACK ISBN: 978-1-6667-3860-5
HARDCOVER ISBN: 978-1-6667-9951-4
EBOOK ISBN: 978-1-6667-9952-1

*Cataloguing-in-Publication data:*

Names: Ahrens, Timothy C., author. Brueggemann, Walter, foreword.

Title: The genius of justice / by Timothy C. Ahrens; foreword by Walter Brueggemann.

Description: Eugene, OR: Cascade Books, 2022.

Identifiers: ISBN 978-1-6667-3860-5 (paperback) | ISBN 978-1-6667-9951-4 (hardcover) | ISBN 978-1-6667-9952-1 (ebook)

Subjects: LCSH: Social justice—Religious aspects—Christianity. | Political activists. | Social reformers—Biography.

Classification: KF373.S75 A50 2022 (print) | KF373 (ebook)

12/02/22

*This book is dedicated to the love of my life,*

*Susan Elizabeth Sitler,*

*who has walked the pathway of justice
all the days of our life together.*

# Contents

## Section 5—The Outward Journey: All Kinds of Justice Doers

## Section 6—Moving Forward: The Drumbeat of Justice

# Foreword

TIM AHRENS IN THIS book has rendered a great service to us. He bears witness to a deep defining hyphen in biblical faith. It is the hyphen that connects *faith* to *justice*: faith-justice! There are of course many modes of faith that arise from the Bible. In the great traditions in Judaism, Christianity, and Islam, there are many different presentations of faith within each tradition. All of these variations, however, share the intent of living from and living back to the living God. There are, in equal fashion, many variant articulations and practices of justice, but in biblical scope all of these variants are *emancipatory, restorative, and redistributive.* The subjects of Tim's book in their various ways all seek to live out this emancipatory, restorative, and redistributive justice that is willed by, authorized by, and empowered by the living God. Thus Moses could declare:

> *Justice, and only justice*, you shall pursue, so that you may live and occupy the land that the Lord our God is giving you (Deuteronomy 16:20).

This mandate is tersely echoed by Jesus:

> For you tithe mint, dill, and cummin, and have neglected the weightier matters of the Torah: *justice, and mercy and faith* (Matthew 23:23).

The accent on this hyphen is crucial because these several faith traditions in practice have an inclination to dissolve the hyphen that makes justice an urgent function of faith. At least in my Christian tradition, the one I know best, we are regularly tempted to reduce faith and its ethic to private personal matters that tilt toward sentimentalism and escapism to the neglect of public issues. Tim shows why that is not possible and points to the conclusion that wherever this hyphen is dissolved two things happen. Justice disappears as an agendum of faith, and faith itself becomes trivial and innocuous.

It is not a surprise that these several lives featured here exhibit justice being enacted and performed in various ways. It is equally not a surprise that all of these venturesome lives are focused and engaged by issues related to *poverty, race, class, and gender.* The exposition that Tim offers show a recurring focus on poverty and on the inescapable "people" outcome for an economy that engages relentlessly in regressive taxation, high interest rates, cheap labor, short-term contracts, temporary jobs, and the exploitation of cheap labor for the ease and comfort of the powerful affluent. The "geniuses" listed here are acutely attentive to the poor who are the unvarying subjects of God's "preferential option."

It is no accident that the willful production of poverty concentrates on minority populations and people of color. We know that racism permeates the entire fabric of our society and has been a root flaw from the inception of our democracy. And not all of the foolish laws banning "critical race theory" will void the requirement that we face, study, and respond to the reality of racism that is everywhere among us. It is, I suggest, a dangerous recognition that some modest progress is being made in the face of racism, because even the most modest progress evokes fresh waves of white supremacy that readily issue violence. And of course the old brands of patriarchy linger in every imaginable way among us, so that women are variously excluded from many parts of our economy, or are penalized by lower wages, or are more generally the carriers of the burdens of an unjust system.

The "geniuses" catalogued here are among those who refuse to accept as "normal" the relentless hostility enacted toward the poor, or to accept the markings of race, class, or gender as signs of privilege, advantage, or superiority. Such nefarious social distinctions can indeed be passed off as "moral" and "normal" only until the God of emancipation, restoration, and redistribution crowds in upon us. That "crowding in" of God does not happen in "supernatural" ways. It happens, rather, because human agents are moved by the reality of God and by the interpretive tradition of faith to host an alternative vision of social relationships, an alternative vision that shows us what is possible and what is mandated, even when it powerfully contradicts our "normal."

What also becomes clear in the testimony of this book is that the systemic insistence upon poverty, race, class, and gender has its endgame in the criminal system and the penal practices of our society. Loic Wacquant, "Crafting the Neoliberal State: Workfare, Prisonfare, and Social Insecurity" (*Sociological Forum* 25.12 (2010) 213) has shown how the penal system is now crucial for the new modes of state craft in our society. That "craft" pertains to:

1. Economic deregulation;

2. Welfare state retraction along with intensification of commodification;

3. An expansive, intrusive, and proactive penal apparatus that is a form of social control over the "unqualified";

4. An endless trope of "individual responsibility" that celebrates those who have "made it."

All of these practices together contribute to the exploitative social apparatus against the vulnerable. Wacquant comments:

> The misery of American welfare and the grandeur of American prisonfare at century's turn are the two sides of the same political coin. The generosity of the latter is in direct proportion to the stinginess of the former, and it expands to the degree that both are driven by moral behaviorism . . . For the punitive containment of urban marginality through the simultaneous rolling back of the social safety net and the rolling out of the police-and-prison dragnet and their knitting together into a carceral-assistential lattice is not the spawn of some broad societal trend—whether it be the ascent of "biopower" or the advent of "late modernity"—but, at bottom, an exercise in *state crafting* (203, 210) (Italics in the original).

It is in this harsh context that these "geniuses" are at work, clearly and boldly, vigorously countercultural, refusing the dominant policies and assumptions of our society, and without apology embracing and practicing the alternative of the kingdom of God.

In her probe of effective presidential leadership Doris Kearns Goodwin (*Leadership in Turbulent Times*) has seen that the great presidents she has studied—including Lincoln, Franklin Roosevelt, and Lyndon Johnson—were masters at combining *transactive work* with *transformative imagination* in a way that increased their effectiveness. My own footnote (Walter Brueggemann, "Twin Themes for Ecumenical Singing," *Journal for Preachers* 43 (Pentecost 2020) 3–10) to Goodwin's discernment is to notice that Psalm 1, with its Torah provisions, and Psalm 2, with its royal expectation, are respectively articulations of *transactive* and *transformative* faith. It is inescapable that our leaders willingly engage in transactive work. Alongside that we are may notice that Tim's "geniuses" are engaged in transformative living, refusing to be contained within the safe reasoning calculus of transaction. Such living requires deep resolve, passionate hope, and street smarts to circumvent and outflank the great force of transactional habits. Thus the work of these "geniuses" is as uncompromisingly transformative was is the covenantal-prophetic tradition of Israel before them. Our faith can only settle for safe transactional practice when it's urgent claims are trivialized or watered down to acceptance. The "geniuses" will have no part in such trivialization, but insist on the full claim of the God of the biblical tradition.

That tradition has forever recognized that the penal system is the end-game of social control by the aggressive powerful. Thus in the great articulation of hope in Isaiah, the poet can give voice to the summons to which these "geniuses" have responded:

He has sent me to bring good news to the oppressed,
to bind up the brokenhearted,
to proclaim liberty to the captives,
and *release to the prisoners;*
to proclaim the year of the Lord's favor,
and the day of vengeance of our God (Isaiah 40:1–2).

The best guess is that these lines proclaim the cancellation of debt as in a year of Jubilee. And in Jesus' parable warning of the end-time, he offers a list of faithful neighborly practices that has prisoners in its purview:

I was hungry and you gave me food, I was thirsty and you gave me something to drink, I was a stranger and you welcomed me, I was naked and you gave me clothing, I was sick and you took care of me, *I was in prison and you visited me* (Matthew 25:35–36).

While a fearful predatory society would prefer to make prisoners invisible, the faith tradition sees them as a community neither forgotten nor disregarded, but taken seriously, even in a society that wants to discard them.

This roster of "geniuses," in sum, reflects a company of transformation. One can see, among these several bold agents, some recurring elements in their lives. They were nurtured in families with an emancipatory perspective, they were early on situated in a peculiar angle of vision so that things are seen differently, they have been often mentored in ways that triggered vision and courage, they grew into a sense of urgency, and they are willing to invest in quite local social reality. These are all ingredients in these transformative lives.

While Tim's scope for identifying "geniuses" is as wide as our entire nation, this is very much a "local" book in Columbus, Ohio. Tim knows this city best where he is an active engaged, transformative pastor. As a result, he is able to identify no less than fourteen "geniuses" in his own local environment. And of course Columbus (along with First Congregational Church where Tim is pastor) is the long-running home base for Washington Gladden, a powerful voice for the Christian social gospel, and a predecessor in the local church to Tim. Besides all of that, Tim himself thrives in Columbus, an effective advocate for the defining hyphen of faith-justice. All of this together suggests that Columbus, the capitol city of Ohio, is singularly blessed by these good agents in justice, perhaps so singular as to be an oddity. But I doubt it! I do not think Columbus is as singular as all of that, even while we may be grateful for all these local "geniuses." It is my suspicion, to the contrary, that if we worked at it attentively, we could find and identify such a presence of "geniuses" in many of our cities and towns. We would find such folk in various locales, because God is at work in many places, as in Columbus, raising up new transformative agents, new advocates, and new witnesses, more than seven thousand of them (see 1 Kings 9:18)! Thus may give thanks for every such locale, and invite those in many venues to take notice of that peculiar community of transformative folk.

The narcotic of a transactional society is that, as it is able, it makes invisible all of those who would most benefit from such transformative imagination and work. And it makes innocuous, as it is able, such agents who place present social arrangements in jeopardy. The word used here for such "sleepiness" is "acedia," spiritual boredom and a lazy acceptance of the status quo. It is the work of religious communities to break the stupor of acedia and to issue "wake-up calls" to the faithful. It must be for that reason that Jesus, in his apocalyptic elusiveness, issues the imperative:

> Therefore *keep awake*—for you do not know when the master of the house will come, in the evening, or at midnight, or at cock-crow, or at dawn, or else he may find you asleep when he comes suddenly. And what I say to you I say to all: *"Keep awake"* (Mark 13:35–37).

Ours is an apocalyptic moment in which God's new justice is breaking in, on the lips and in the lives of many faithful people. The "geniuses" embody an "alarm clock" for the rest of us, issuing an alarm and calling us to wake up to the alternative governance that is on the move among us.

It may be hoped that this rich, suggestive book will be for many of us a summons and an invitation to an alternative life, one filled with the juices of neighborly justice. This book teems with hope concerning alternative social possibility. We have sufficient resources for a neighborly community; all that is missing is the political will to act. Hope is the ground for such political will. Wherever that hope is taken seriously, it yields a different life. These "geniuses" respond, as the faithful have always responded, to the imperative of the apostle:

> Do not be conformed to this world, but be transformed by the renewing of your minds, so that you may discern what the will of God—what is is good and acceptable and perfect (Romans 12:2).

## Walter Brueggemann

Columbia Theological Seminary
March 16, 2022

# Acknowledgments

*"Where there is no vision, the people perish . . ."*

PROVERBS 29:18

I THANK GOD EACH day that I am alive and able to fight for justice and stand up and speak out for what is right and good in this world. I am grateful every day to serve as a pastor and faith leader in Ohio.

I am deeply grateful for so many people who have contributed to this project. Before the Genius of Justice Project took off, Doug Kridler, Dr. Lynn Wallich, Ray Miller, and the Dominican Sisters of Peace believed in the vision. Thank you for believing in this vision and supporting me in so many ways for so many years.

Sr. Simone Campbell, SSS was the first genius to speak with me in early June 2021. She helped the nebulous void take shape and form. She helped me believe there was something here. Throughout the project, Sr. Simone supported my efforts and raised important questions—all rising from her heart of prayer. Across the summer of 2021, people answered their emails and phones and opened themselves up to conversations. All fifty-three geniuses of justice are a blessing to my life. I am grateful for them and all around them who helped our conversations happen. I am especially grateful to Walter and Tia Brueggemann who welcomed me and supported my efforts throughout this project. Thank you Walter for the forward to this book and your inspiration to my life and ministry.

Thank you to all my friends, staff, and members of First Congregational United Church of Christ, Columbus, Ohio, who supported me through the research and writing phase of this project. A special thanks goes to Nancy Braverman and Dani Ahrens for their work on the project. Thank you to the entire staff of Cascade Books and especially my editor Rodney Clapp for all your support and direction through this publishing process.

Thank you to my four adult children, Luke, Dani, Thalia, and Sarah, and their beloved ones, Kirsten, Alilie, Adam, and Nathan, and my seven grandchildren, Benton, Ethan, Rylan, Aaden, Emryn, Axel, and Hazel for your constant love. You are all so beautiful and I love you so much. Thanks as well to my sister and brother, Deb and Paul, and especially my mother, Lorene Kellermeyer Ahrens, who has supported me my whole life long. Thank you from here to eternity for my father, Dr. Herman C. Ahrens Jr., who inspired me through the depths of his faith to read, write, ask questions, seek answers, tell the truth about injustice, and fight nonviolently for justice.

Most of all, I thank God for Susan Elizabeth Sitler, my spouse and the love of my life. You have stood by me, and walked with me through everything we have faced since November 9, 1985. Together we have been inspired by Edmond Burke's words, "the only thing necessary for the triumph of evil is for good men to do nothing." In this effort, you gave me time and space to research, interview, read, write, and edit this book. Thank you for all your love and support all the days of our life together.

# Section 1—**Understanding the Genius of Justice**

# Chapter 1: The "It" Factor in a Justice Genius

*"The arc of the moral universe is long, but it bends towards justice."*

—THEODORE PARKER

AMINAH BRENDA LYNN ROBINSON was a genius. Her eyes witnessed and her hands shaped and told the stories of her heart. With fabric and paint, textiles and buttons she made simple objects and huge mixed media assemblages as, through her art, she celebrated family, ancestors, and the stuff of life in the African American community of my home—Columbus, Ohio.

In 2004, the MacArthur Foundation recognized Aminah's genius as a folk artist and awarded her a MacArthur Fellowship grant. I happened to be in the Columbus Museum of Art the day a representative of the MacArthur Foundation was having lunch with her. Aminah saw me, rose from her chair, and said, "Tim, I am a genius and I'm rich!" Then she explained her victory. She was indeed richer than she had ever been and, as always—she was a genius.

Aminah died on May 22, 2015. I think of her often. Knowing her influenced me deeply. One of my favorite geniuses in Columbus was one of our nation's best-kept artist secrets. She was able to see the world through the lens of people's lives and their daily reality. She told their stories through the years. She saw the beauty and joy, the pain and perseverance in people's lives, and she shared it all through her brilliant and colorful artistic creations.

The spirit of Aminah Brenda Lynn Robinson has guided my heart in this Genius of Justice Project. Through Aminah, I have come to know what a genius looks like. Through the lens of her life, I have looked at my colleagues, friends, inspired national leaders, and the sages of faith and justice and I have seen their genius, too.

There are geniuses in every field of work and life, born in every age. I happen to work and live in the field of faith. This is where the crop of geniuses that I know grow and thrive. Across my lifetime, I have been blessed with their power and presence in faith communities across the globe. Frederick Douglass, Sojourner Truth, Harriet Tubman, Mahatma Gandhi, Martin Luther King Jr., Fred Shuttlesworth, John Lewis, Howard Thurman, Abraham Joshua Heschel, James Lawson, and so many more have changed the way we see the world and how we make change in the world. Each one of these gifted leaders has been a genius of justice.

I believe there are geniuses of justice in this world today.

These geniuses of justice are women and men whose brilliance reflects the distinctive power and ability to influence others to change something. As I have noted, we find geniuses in all fields of work and life. I will focus on predominantly faith-based justice geniuses in Jewish and Christian traditions. These are my people. This is my wheelhouse. As an interfaith leader, I have come to know these folks and been touched by their genius of justice across my lifetime.

I define **genius** as a character of spirit that embodies the best—or sometimes the worst—of human nature. A genius has a strongly marked capacity or aptitude which that person uses effectively and well. The "justice geniuses" use their excellence to influence and change people, policies, and the times in which they live. Throughout time, **justice** has been important to our Christian faith and people of all faiths. From the earliest writings of the Hebrew poets and prophets and through the ministry of Jesus and through the ages of Jewish and Christian sages, justice has been a central demand and call of our Jewish and Christian faiths.

In the summer of 2021, I listened to and learned from the women and men whom I have come to believe are "geniuses" in the work of social justice. I heard their "call" stories and their life stories. I found out what angers them and what wakes them up in the middle of night. What inspires them to take justice action for others? Who inspires them? What is their source of renewal and restoration? In other words, how do they not get burned out in their pursuit of justice? For many of them, I wondered, how have they spent their lifetimes committed to biblically grounded justice ministry?

As I learned their stories and now share them with you, some of their genius will simply appear to be "best practices" for all of life. Other elements of their genius will have distinctive characteristics. My hope is that this project will inspire you and others to find and claim your own inner justice genius. I hope you are inspired to stand up, speak out, and do the right thing in the face of injustice. I want you to make this world a better place for all people and all creation.

During the ebbs and flows of the COVID-19 pandemic, I engaged in fifty-three conversations with geniuses of justice—some well-known, some lesser known. Some are national figures who soar through headlines and news stories of our times as they write, march, preach, and inspire tens of thousands of people. Some of them work quietly in small parishes and synagogues. Some are scholars, lawyers, medical doctors, and activists who are behind the scenes fighting for the end of injustice.

All fifty-three have that special "it" factor, which I saw on Zoom or face-to-face. Each of the fifty-three geniuses of justice have a drive and deep desire to overcome the disorder of this world and set us right again. Each cares deeply about this earth, about the people of this earth and treating people right. Each believes in making it possible for people to have a chance to thrive. They believe in leveling the playing field so that the narrative of our lives and times is about abundance and not scarcity; about justice and not inequity.

Cornel West has written, "Justice is what love looks like in public." These geniuses of justice are lovers of others in public as they dig in to do justice. They speak the truth.

One day while out walking my dogs, Dug and Charlie, I stopped and wrote this about the fifty-three:

> A genius of justice doesn't apologize for justice. They don't use the word in the back half of a sentence, in a whisper, with a question mark. They lead with justice. It rolls off their tongues like Amos's waters "flowing down like righteousness." Justice is not a secondary thought or emotion. It is not an afterthought. It is always a forethought. Justice doesn't trouble, it informs. Justice is strategic. It is always communal. It is always personal. A genius of justice sees a person who others have not seen. She hears the person who has not been heard. He walks with a person who has had no one who walked by their side for years. A genius of justice is humble yet focused. A genius of justice is merciful in their kindness.

The geniuses of justice answer their phones. They educate and elucidate. They cross lines of race, gender, class, sexual orientation, and more to build coalitions and relationships. Their creativity leads them to look inside out at problems and then solve them. Some of them hate the word genius because all social change is collective and collaborative and it is not about being a genius. This belief is half true. Social change is always collaborative, but it takes a vision to bring it into reality. They believe salvation is not simply about personal salvation but always about social salvation. They are good at confronting and dealing with liars, tricksters, and terrorists.

They are just women and men; Jewish, Christian, people of all religions, spiritual but not religious, Black, white, and brown, straight, gay, nonbinary, old and young. The fifty-three reside in sixteen different states, Washington, DC, and Tel Aviv, Israel. Some are sages and some are practical practitioners. Some have come to the work of justice hesitantly and accidentally. Some were raised in homes where activism was a course served at dinner each night and twice on the Sabbath day. Some were brought along through injustices faced at an early age because of the color of their skin and the zip code of their apartment or house. Some lost a brother or a son to gun violence and were brought to their knees and then to their feet to fight for justice. One barely survived war in the rice paddies and jungles of Viet Nam and rose to become a leader in my city. Some were educated into justice battles through experiences or learning in high school or college. Some were persecuted and beaten because they were Black in all-white schools. Some were bullied, tormented, and persecuted because they were gay in a world that is violent and vile in its treatment of LGBTQ children, teens, and adults. Some are phenomenal musicians, singers, and recording artists. Most read the Holy Scripture and are motivated to do justice because God has called them to do it. Some can't tell anything about any Scripture but they know the law and medicine and live by the Golden Rule and the moral code of their profession. Some work on the streets and in soup kitchens with the homeless poor and some of them are champions for new generations of new Americans or newly poor people in America.

All of them, in my mind, have the certain "it" factor that makes them geniuses of justice. They see "it." They feel "it." They wake with "it" on their heart and mind and fall asleep at night exhausted from the battle. They fight to change what is wrong. Years ago, I heard Joseph Campbell tell a story in the PBS series *The Power of Myth*. It's the story of a fellow who turns the corner and sees a brawl in the middle of the block. He runs right for it, shouting: "Is this a private fight, or can anyone get in it?"

The geniuses of justice are nonviolent warriors who fight for others that have been knocked to the ground or have their backs pinned against a wall. They believe in democracy and freedom so strongly that they jump in the fight to make this nation and world a better place. I am not talking about fistfights and violent attacks on others. Rather, I am talking about the battle for justice in which confrontation leads to change. They know that the power of people working together to change what is wrong can shift the direction of injustice and evil and turn it to the right course. They know that organizing people for justice can correct the direction of policies that defy the common good and common sense and leave children and families bereft and suffering. They do the right thing and they do it well.

They have a twinkle in their eyes and a hop in their steps. They have steel in their spines. They have hands that open to serve and lift and carry people. They don't seem to tire as they work tirelessly for the "tired poor." They listen intently and act compassionately. They have powerful preaching and singing voices. They are leaders when the moment calls to lead and they follow when they are called to follow. They open their hearts and minds to the possibility and vision of a better world for all. They follow the voice of their God and the inspiration of their ancestors. They know what is right and what is wrong. They do not yield in the face of what is wrong. They never give up. They never give in. They live in hope even on bad days.

## Here are the Fifty-Three Geniuses of Justice:

- Dr. Amy Acton—executive director, RAPID 5, and former medical director for the state of Ohio during 2020's COVID-19 pandemic, Columbus, Ohio.

- Rev. John Aeschbury—executive director, Direct Action Research Training (DART), Miami, Florida; resides in Columbus, Ohio.

- Dr. Robert Bilott—author and partner, Taft Stettinius & Hollister, LLP, Covington, Kentucky.

- Dr. Walter Brueggemann—William Marcellus McPheeters Professor of Old Testament emeritus at Columbia Theological Seminary, Decatur, Georgia, who now resides in Traverse City, Michigan.

- Rev. Dr. Jennifer Butler—author, founder and CEO of Faith in Public Life, Washington, DC.

- Sr. Simon Campbell, SSS—author and executive director emeritus, NETWORK, Washington, DC.

- Rev. Dr. Tony Campolo—author, professor emeritus of sociology and leading evangelical, Eastern Baptist University, St. David's, Pennsylvania.

- Cantor Jack Chomsky—cantor emeritus, Congregation Tifereth Israel, Columbus, Ohio, who now resides in Tel Aviv, Israel.

- Pastor Shane Claiborne—Christian activist, author, pastor of the Simple Way Community, Philadelphia, Pennsylvania.

- Rev. Dan Clark—executive director, Faith in Public Life–Ohio, Columbus, Ohio.

- Dr. Marian Wright Edelman—author and founder, CEO emeritus, Children's Defense Fund, Washington DC.

- Rev. John Edgar—CEO emeritus, Community Development for All People, pastor emeritus, Church for All People, Columbus, Ohio.

- Fr. Phil Egitto—pastor, Our Lady of Lourdes Catholic Church, Daytona Beach, Florida.

- Bishop Yvette Flunder—senior pastor, City of Refuge United Church of Christ, Oakland, California.

- Mr. Terry "Nunnie" Green—founder and CEO, "Think Make Live Youth," Columbus, Ohio.

- Rev. Dr. J. Bennett Guess—executive director of the Ohio ACLU, Columbus/Cleveland, Ohio.

- Rev. Dr. Obrey M. Hendricks Jr.—professor of religion and African American studies, Columbia University, New York City.

- Dr. Susannah Heschel—The Eli M. Black Distinguished Professor of Jewish Studies at Dartmouth College, Hanover, New Hampshire.

- Rev. Charles Heyward—senior pastor emeritus, St. James Presbyterian Church, James Island, South Carolina.

- Rev. Ralph Hodge—senior pastor, Second Baptist Church, South Richmond, Virginia.

- Fr. Chris Hoffman—pastor, Our Lady of the Lakes Catholic Church, Deltona, Florida.

- Minister Adrienne Hood—minister, True Love Ministries, Columbus, Ohio.

- Rev. Dr. Jefferey P. Kee—senior pastor, New Faith Baptist Church of Christ, Columbus, Ohio.

- Rabbi Rick Kellner—senior rabbi, Congregation Beth Tikvah, Columbus, Ohio.

- Marty Kress—retired, Ohio State University, Columbus, Ohio.

- Rabbi Seth M. Limmer—author and senior rabbi, Chicago Sinai Congregation, Chicago, Illinois.

- Rev. Dr. Ron Luckey—retired Lutheran pastor, Lexington, Kentucky.

- Rev. Sarah Marsh—mercy and justice coordinator (of the Great Plains Conference of the United Methodist Church), Lawrence, Kansas.

- Lt. Melissa Weems McFadden—author and lieutenant, Columbus Division of Police, Columbus, Ohio.

- Ruth Messinger—president/CEO, American Jewish World Service, New York City.

- Rev. Dr. Otis Moss Jr.—pastor emeritus, Olivet Institutional Baptist Church (1975–2008), Cleveland, Ohio.

- Rev. Dr. Otis Moss III—senior pastor, Trinity United Church of Christ, Chicago, Illinois.

- Fr. Dan Noll—pastor, Mary Queen of the Holy Rosary Parish, Lexington, Kentucky.

- Sr. Margaret Ormond, OP—retired president, Dominican Academy, former prioress, Dominican Sisters of Peace, Columbus, Ohio.

- Rev. Dr. Joseph L. Owens—senior pastor, Shiloh Baptist, Lexington, Kentucky.

- Rev. Robert Owens—founder and lead organizer, Citizens of Louisville Organized and United Together (CLOUT), Louisville, Kentucky.

- Dr. John M. Perkins—author, speaker, and president emeritus of the John and Vera Mae Perkins Foundation, Jackson, Mississippi.

- Rabbi Jonah Dov Pesner—author and director, Religious Action Center of Reform Judaism, and senior vice president of the Union for Reform Judaism, Washington, DC.

- Rev. Dr. Ray Pickett—New Testament theologian and scholar, rector, Pacific Lutheran Theological Seminary, Berkeley, California.

- Rev. Loey Powell—retired United Church of Christ pastor, Cleveland, Ohio.

- Sr. Helen Prejean—CSJ, Congregation of St. Joseph, author and executive director, Ministry Against the Death Penalty, Baton Rouge, Louisiana.

- Congressman Rev. Dr. Bobby Rush—representative, First Congressional District, Illinois, and Senior Pastor, Beloved Community Church of God in Christ, Chicago, Illinois.

- Rabbi David Saperstein—director and chief legal counsel emeritus, The Union for Reform Judaism's Religious Action Center.

- Bishop Lafayette Scales—senior pastor, Rhema Christian Fellowship, Columbus, Ohio.

- Fr. John Tapp—pastor, Holy Family Church, St. Petersburg, Florida.

- Thomas Terp—chairman and managing partner, Taft Stettinius & Hollister, LLP, Cincinnati, Ohio.

- Rev. Dr. Liz Theoharis—author and co-director, The Poor People's Campaign, New York City.

- Rev. Dr. Susan Thistlethwaite—president emeritus/professor of theology, Chicago Theological Seminary, residing in Aspen, Colorado.

- Rabbi Rachel Timoner—author and senior rabbi, Congregation Beth Elohim, Brooklyn, New York.

- Bishop Donald J. Washington—senior pastor, Mt. Hermon Missionary Baptist Church, Columbus, Ohio.

- Rev. Dr. Cindy Weber—pastor, Jeff St. Baptist Community Church at Liberty, Louisville, Kentucky.

- Rev. Dr. Starsky Wilson—executive director, Children's Defense Fund, Washington, DC.

- Rev. Dr. Jeremiah Wright—author and senior pastor emeritus, Trinity United Church of Christ, Chicago, Illinois.

I want to mention four more geniuses of justice with whom I attempted to converse, but despite many efforts, was unable to meet: Rev. Dr. William J. Barber, II, Dr. Ibram X. Kendi, Bryan Stevenson, and Isabel Wilkerson. Each is in my daily prayers and find their way into this book by the sheer power of their influence on my life and our world. I am grateful to God for each one.

In the following pages you will meet these geniuses in various ways. I cannot do justice to the depth and breadth of their achievements. What I can do is share the wisdom and experiences and the spirit with which they move and have their being.

These are truly amazing women and men. Find ways to engage them, meet them, read their writings, listen to their preaching, worship in the churches and synagogues where they serve. You will be inspired. You will be changed. Moreover, I hope and pray their inspiration will move you to pray more deeply, act more clearly for justice, and make a difference in this world, wherever you are located.

I give you this prayer, written by Sr. Maxine Shonk, OP, and appearing in her book of prayers, *Silver Linings: Blessings for Shadow Times* (2012). It is the prayer with which I opened every conversation with the geniuses of justice. It is meant to be a blessing for you, too.

> May God's spirit bless you when you see or experience injustice. May you be overtaken with a passion for truth as you guard and preserve your own integrity. May you **stand up** for those without voice, **stand in** for the victims of oppression and discrimination, and **stand out** in your persistence and desire for God's peace and justice in the world. May you live your life in pursuit of truth and in profound reverence for all of God's creation. May the God of JUSTICE bless you always.

May the God of justice *truly* bless you always.

Let us commence in this journey with the geniuses of justice.

### Reflection to Action Questions:

1. Do you know anyone who has the "it" factor as a genius of justice in your life? How do they inspire you to step up and take action for justice?

2. What characteristics of the geniuses of justice mentioned in this chapter resonate with your spirit? How are they common to other inspirational people in your life? How are they different?

3. Make a list of the characteristics you have that give you a certain "it" factor in facing and dealing with injustice in this world.

# Section 2—**The Ground on Which We Stand for Justice**

# Chapter 2: **Close to God—The Text and Prophetic Imagination**

*Let justice roll down like waters and righteousness
like an ever-flowing stream.*

—Amos 5:24

SOMETIME IN THE AUTUMN of 755 BCE, the prophet Amos was speaking God's word to people who refused to listen. Stopping by a worship center, probably the place called Bethel, and unloading his brutally frank "Word of the Lord," Amos's message totally rejected the worship of the people. Clearly, the Lord despised and hated the people's feasts, their solemn assemblies, their burnt offerings, their cereal offerings, their peace offerings, and their melody and noise (can you hear all the noise?).

God disdained the sights, the smells, the words, and the sounds of their worship. Through Amos, God cleansed the sensory nightmare his people offered as worship. God sought justice and righteousness as true worship! God saw that there was no communion with the Holy One, only commotion in the holy place, and the Lord demanded an end to that garbage.

God spoke through the prophets of old. Abraham Joshua Heschel understood this. He wrote in *The Prophets*:

> The prophet is a person who sees the world with the eyes of God, who holds God and humanity in one thought, at one time, in all times . . . The passion of God is speaking when the prophet speaks. . . . He feels fiercely. God has thrust a burden upon his soul and he is bowed and stunned by humanity's fierce greed . . . Prophecy is the voice that God has lent to the silent agony, a voice to the plundered poor, to the profaned riches of the world. It is a form of living, a crossing point of God and man. God is raging in the prophet's words . . . The prophet seldom tells a story, but casts events. . . . He lives in sympathy with the divine pathos.

15

God's justice—spoken through the prophets—has three dimensions.

First, God's justice is dynamic. It is not the justice that balances scales judiciously—as portrayed by the blindfolded woman holding the scales of justice. God's justice is the moving, torrential justice that rushes down until injustice is swept away! It is God's voice "lent to the silent agony" of this world. God's justice is never at rest. It is moving forward in power and in truth. It will not be silenced, neither will it be subdued. God's justice is dynamic.

Second, God expects justice as the response to what God has done for people. Simply stated, doing justice is what you and I are expected to do for God. The pattern of divine indicative followed by expected human response runs throughout the Bible. For example, God delivers the chosen people out of bondage and in so doing God lays out expectations for them in the Ten Commandments. In the letter to the Romans, Paul begins with an exposition of the gospel in chapters 1–11, followed by suggestions for the expected response to that good news in chapters 12–16. In Colossians, the meaning of the Christ event is explained from the first verse of chapter one through 3:4 with imperatives following in the rest of the letter. In the words of 1 John 4:19: "We love, because God first loved us!" Our God expects justice as our response to what God has done for us!

Third, God's justice requires action. This is big for God! God's justice is not still. To do justice is to act as advocates and defenders of the powerless. In Amos, Isaiah, Deuteronomy, and throughout Hebrew Scriptures, "to seek justice" means to advocate on behalf of the poor, the orphan, and the widow. When the prophets of old speak of justice, there is nothing theoretical, nothing philosophical, nothing even legal in their notions.

The spirits of prophets of old are with us still. In their new manifestation, God is still speaking in the prophets of our times who lead us out of the halls of worship into quarters of the town or city where the poor live. They command us to look into the eyes of the lonely widow, the hurting orphan, the hungry and homeless man. They demand that we listen to and respond to the medically fragile, the housing unstable, and the food-denied sisters and brothers at our doors and lost on the streets of our villages, towns, and cities. They implore us to see and respond to the abused and neglected child, the unfairly paid immigrant, the forsaken, the forlorn, and the forgotten. We have to see those in need and respond as powerful people for God.

The prophets of our times say to us now and forevermore, "Justice now! Justice always! Let justice roll down like an ever-flowing stream!"

God is still speaking through prophets of our time.

We know that God was speaking in the story of Luke 4:14–21. We know the Spirit of God as given to the prophet Isaiah came unraveled one day in the synagogue of Nazareth. A young Jewish prophet, baptized with river water by John and baptized in wilderness fires of temptation by Satan, came home to worship—as he always did on the Sabbath. His name was Jesus.

As the scroll was passed to Jesus, he dutifully read what was placed before him. The words were these from Isaiah 61:1ff:

> The spirit of the Lord is upon me, because God has anointed me, to preach good news to the poor, God has sent me to proclaim release to the captives, and recovering of sight to the blind, to set at liberty those who oppressed, to proclaim the acceptable year of the Lord.

Good news to the poor, healing, release (or *forgiveness* as the Greek often translates) from various kinds of captivity, and proclamation of Jubilee all become themes of Jesus' ministry and teaching. Was it coincidence or was it a "God-speaking" incident that brought this text before Jesus? I believe it was God still speaking through Jesus.

No matter how we interpret that moment, Isaiah 61:1ff was the perfect scriptural selection for the Spirit-filled and anointed son of the Nazarene synagogue. But God was not finished speaking when the scroll was laid down. Jesus sat down and continued to speak in prophetic ways that nearly costs him his life by stoning to death when he added, "Today the scriptures have been fulfilled in your hearing."

"Fulfilling the Scripture" is actually the call for all who walk in the ways of faith-filled justice. It is not enough to read the Bible. It is not enough to offer clear and concise exegetical references and interpretations, so that folks nod in agreement (or perhaps nod off in a catatonic sleep state).

God knows, people need fulfillment of Scripture. God knows, people need the Spirit upon them and within them. God knows, the poor need good news! God knows, people need to be healed of the pain they carry around daily from losses they have experienced, from depression they have battled, from injuries they have sustained in life's walk. God knows, people need forgiveness of sins, forgiveness of debts, forgiveness of burdens, forgiveness of foolish words spoken and strange behaviors acted upon. God knows, people need to be released from captivity—whether physical, mental, spiritual, or emotional. God knows, those blinded, for whatever reason, need to see again. God knows, the Spirit of God is needed for fulfillment—not just one more reading of one more ancient text.

God is still speaking. God will not be silent. God will not sit down and look the other way. God will not turn away from the needs of God's children. And wherever, and whenever, and however justice is done, the garbage of injustice is washed away, healing and forgiveness happen, captives are released, the blind see again, the joy of Jubilee is fulfilled, and the beautiful feet of the prophets take to the streets, the plains, the seasides, and the mountaintops of this world—*God is still speaking.*

Isaiah 40:21–22 asks:

> Have you not known? Have you not heard? Has it not been told you from the beginning? Have you not understood from the foundation of the earth? It is God who sits above the circle of the earth ... and God who makes the rulers of the earth for nothing.

As the prophets speak today, we must listen and respond as well.

In my project, I reached out and listened to the geniuses of justice who daily live inside the ancient texts of Scripture and teachings. I needed to hear from the biblically centered prophets of our time who drill down into the language, spirit, and essence of the Bible and share the depth of their discoveries with us. Five people came to mind. They teach the prophets in Jewish and Christian Scriptures and have drawn inspiration and hope from the insights of prophetic imagination.

These scholars are: Rev. Dr. Walter Brueggemann, Rev. Dr. Obrey M. Hendricks Jr., Rev. Dr. Ray Pickett, Dr. Susannah Heschel, and Rev. Dr. Susan Brooks Thistlethwaite. They are wise and gifted in addressing biblical justice. They have written on issues of economics and consumerism, the idolatry of money power, militarism and nationalism, moral action in the real world, the politics of Jesus, the prophets in Jewish and Christian Scriptures, the intersection of Jewish/Christian relations, and a range of other issues of faith in public life.

Through the years, each has directly addressed the corruption of the Christian church or Jewish leaders when they lose their way and miss the call to serve God through prophetic justice witness. Each comes to their scholarly labor as a person of faith. Their faith informs their scholarship and their scholarship informs all of us as people of faith seeking to do justice in this world. In the course of our conversations, each brought faithful insights to our current conditions as a nation and a world.

Walter Brueggemann has authored more than fifty-eight books, nineteen commentaries on the Bible, and hundreds of articles. Now retired, he is the William Marcellus McPheeters Professor of Old Testament emeritus at Columbia Theological Seminary in Decatur, Georgia. His book *The Prophetic Imagination*, first published in 1978, has become a handbook for biblical social justice clergy and laity. Since then, it has inspired and guided the biblical foundation and faith-based social justice witness for generations of people of faith.

When we sat together in his home in Traverse City, Michigan, I asked Walter what or who inspires his work for social justice. His answer was simply, "The Text. It keeps energizing me with the dramatic examples of individual persons who step out and make a difference." Foolishly I pressed, "Any particular text?" He answered with a smile, "All the Text." By the Text, he was not referring to something that popped up on his iPhone. He was speaking about "*the* Text" of Holy Scripture—the entire Bible.

All of the Bible has inspired Walter Brueggemann all his life. Together, we walked through the story of his life, beginning March 11, 1933 in Tilden, Nebraska. Walter was one of two proud sons of a pastor in the German Evangelical Synod of North America, the forerunner of the current United Church of Christ. Of his mother he said, "she would have been a pastor in another generation." Of his father he said, "my dad was on the right side of the justice questions. He was not outspoken or aggressive. He worked on it in quiet ways that I understood." Growing up, the church was the epicenter of his life. Nurtured in the faith of German pietism based in mercy, compassion, and caring for others, he grew up in poor, rural communities in Nebraska and Missouri. From the sixth grade on, he lived in Blackburn, Missouri. "We had a small Black community in my town. My brother and I were the janitors at the Black school and we could see up close the injustices the Black community faced."

It was at Elmhurst College that his moral passion connected to justice as he studied sociology with Dr. Theophil W. Mueller. Dr. Mueller was an outspoken advocate for justice. He taught about race, class conflict, the distribution of power, and the balance of justice. Brueggemann was so inspired by Dr. Mueller that he became a sociology major. At Eden Seminary he was turned on to the Old Testament and was "channeled into Old Testament studies" that fueled his passion for justice. Once there, the justice questions were "inescapable." At Union Seminary in New York, under the tutelage of James Muhlenberg, Brueggemann gained the skills for rhetorical criticism that, in his words, "emancipated the text." It would be ten years as a professor at Eden Seminary in St. Louis, Missouri before Walter felt emboldened to write. Following a series of lectures to clergy, he turned it into a book. He never stopped writing once he started. Thanks be to God!

Walter's love of justice comes out when he speaks of his passion for "the Text." When teaching about justice in the Scriptures he says, "I was a patient teacher. I would slow down and walk them through the text. Seeing justice in the entire Bible is not only legitimate, it is inescapable . . . Once you understand class conflict, the Bible is all about the 'haves' and the 'have nots.'"

He continues, "Prophetic imagination is the capacity to entertain a world other than the one that is in front of us. It seems to me that is exactly what the Bible wants us to do. It invites us to host a world other than the one we see."

Walter says, "Justice is the task of apportioning the abundant common good so that every member can live a life of dignity and security. It is distributive justice. The great justice story is the manna story in which the abundant common good is available to all but it cannot be stored up. Jesus in the two feeding miracles reiterates the manna story. The Eucharist reiterates the manna story. The accent of creation faith is on the abundance of God which contradicts the programmatic scarcity of the capitalistic system. While it wasn't capitalism, the adversaries of the prophets all lived by the scarcity system. We are all schooled in the scarcity system."

What makes Walter angry is to witness injustice in our time. He said, "Injustice is the eclipse of human connectedness in the service of fear and greed. This has many manifestations. How can we be so obtuse to engage in so much self-destruction when we know better? How can we be so self-serving in so many shameless ways? In the words of Jeremiah, 'you no longer know how to be ashamed.' If you no longer know how to be ashamed, school is out."

Walter Brueggemann wrote many years ago in a little book on Micah 6:8, "Justice is finding out what belongs to whom and returning it to them." This is illustrated in the Jubilee Year, which concerns giving stuff back to people who have lost it.

Brueggemann lives in the spirit of God and with the heart and mind of prophetic imagination. He has gifted us with his poetic and powerful presence since the first time he picked up a pen and shared his reflections and insights into "the Text"—the whole text.

Susannah Heschel is an author and the Eli M. Black Distinguished Professor of Jewish Studies at Dartmouth College. She sees the need to come together across the many divisions of our times. She told me, "We need to be daring. We need to feel something other than anger and find ways to have respectful conversations. We need to be at dinner tables with those who are different than we are and find our common ground." Dr. Heschel has written about intersection of Jewish and Christian relations through history. She talked of the connections between German theologians from the 1890s on paying little to no attention to the Hebrew prophets, with famed theologian Ernst Troeltsch even calling the prophets "country bumpkins." The shame of this ignorance forged a foundation that allowed the rise of Nazi "theologians" by the 1930s.

She emphasized that God's revelation always has a twofold function. First, it is the Word that God gives to us. Second, it is the Word that we receive from God. So that which is given by God must also be received by God's people. The questions she asks are: "Are we up to the challenge with the Bible? Can we handle it? Can we receive what God has given us?"

We also spoke about the prophets and friendship, particularly about the friendship between her father, Jewish theologian Abraham Joshua Heschel, and Rev. Dr. Martin Luther King Jr. Susannah has written of that relationship: "The friendship between Heschel and King was unusual in its day, and was surprising to many, but also inspiring because the two came from such different backgrounds and yet found intimacy that grew out of their religious commitments and transcended the growing public rifts between their two communities. Heschel brought King and his message to a wide Jewish audience and King made Heschel a central figure in the struggle for civil rights."

Heschel and King were both prophets in their own rights. King was the prophetic preacher and pastor. Heschel was the prophetic preacher and scholar. Both blended their prophetic gifts in powerful ways to address injustice. Together, they formed a dynamic duo of prophecy and truthtelling. In June 1963, when called to the White House to meet with President John F. Kennedy and Dr. King, Heschel sent a telegram the day before the meeting calling the president to declare a "State of Moral Emergency." Continuing, he said, "The hour calls for moral grandeur and spiritual audacity." A few months later on the steps of the Lincoln Memorial, Heschel was with Dr. King as King delivered his "I Have a Dream" speech.

When I asked Dr. Susannah Heschel about her father and Dr. King, she spoke with great love and affection for both men. She spoke of their deep friendship in the last years of King's life. She said, "Dr. King was always sincere and gracious in our home. He was genuinely interested in what I was studying, reading, and writing. He was friendly and kind and was always welcomed as a family member in my home."

Dr. Brueggemann and Dr. Heschel have had a primary focus on the Hebrew Scriptures and Jewish/Christian encounter with texts and one another. Dr. Susan Brooks Thistlethwaite, Dr. Obrey Hendricks Jr., and Rev. Dr. Ray Pickett have primarily focused on Christian Scriptures as biblical scholars and theologians.

Susan Brooks Thistlethwaite is professor of theology emerita and president emerita at Chicago Theological Seminary. Citing her Hungarian ancestry and her DNA fingerprints of resistance to oppression, Susan shared her lifelong struggle for justice for all. When men from her high school went to Viet Nam, they were heralded with a wall listing their names. As the war ground on and the deaths kept mounting new names were not added and recognition of the other names was forgotten. She and other students carried their names around the school.

At Smith College, she left the Lutheranism of her childhood and joined the United Church of Christ. She was active in the women's movement and shared that when people told her, "You can't do this," it was "like waving a red flag in front of a bull!" At Duke University, she was in a seminary with 250 men and four women. She and others were told that women's concerns and issues had to take a back seat to racism and liberation theology and she rose up and said, "No!" Her resistance led her to work with women who experienced domestic violence. It also led her to write about women's bodies as battlefields in the violent, abusive war against women. She pastored, preached, wrote, and taught women's studies and theology and was involved on the Task Force for the National Council of Churches, which produced the first inclusive language lectionary for the Christian church.

Beginning in 1984, Susan called Chicago home as a professor and president of Chicago Theological Seminary. Her insights into justice are well documented and published. Her contributions to public theology have gained her a national following far beyond the walls of the academy and church. She is quotable and relatable for everyone and anyone.

During our conversation, Susan shared a number of aphoristic and penetrating quotes, including the following:

- "War is dumb. War after war we know this is true. I already oppose the next war."

- "You can't see justice unless you are in the streets. All justice comes from movements of change."

- "Justice is never an abstraction. It is always real and personal."

- "Fear is also never an abstraction. It too is real in people's lives."

- "Those who oppress always want to shut you up. If you shut up, they've got you."

- "People who have never experienced structural or systematic oppression protest masks and claim they are expressing their freedom. But they are—in fact—adding to the pain of those who are on the margins."

- "We who are white must try to clean ourselves out to the core because racism is so much a part of how we function in this world."

- "In order to be an activist, you have to let the everyday events of this world affect you and change you."

- "You have to feel the poison that whiteness brings to cleanse it from your system."

- "Each of us needs to make room every day for new news."

- "You know justice by its absence."

- "If we followed the United Nations Universal Declaration of Human Rights, justice would reign in this world because the essence of biblical truth and justice action is reflected in this document."

Thistlethwaite has a clarion voice in the prophetic imagination of our times. She has shaken the foundations of common beliefs and practices in church and academy. Like Esther, she has risen for such a time as this to push us out of our comfort zones and into the public square.

Rev. Dr. Obrey Hendricks Jr. is an author, activist, religious scholar, and professor of religion and African American studies at Columbia University and a visiting professor of Bible and ethics at Union Theological Seminary. In his latest book, *Christians Against Christianity: How Right-Wing Evangelicals Are Destroying Our Nation and Our Faith* (2021), he takes aim at right-wing evangelical Christians who have moved from preaching and teaching an admirable faith to embracing a pernicious, destructive ideology.

He is a hands-on prophet. With time spent in the Black nationalist movement, as a student of Karl Marx, and as a trader on Wall Street, Hendricks is bringing experience, plus fire and the Spirit as he writes, teaches, and lives out a prophetic witness in this world. The challenges he sees in the current trending toward the end of democracy reminds him of Nazism eighty years ago. He is concerned that if we don't turn this around now, our children and grandchildren will have nothing left to call America. The hypocrisy and lies right-wing leaders are projecting will lead to the destruction of democracy—all done in the name of Jesus. All of this has deep racist underpinnings as well. Besides his powerful prophetic punch, Obrey is a boxer and has been for years. He can deliver more than words as he powers through life.

Obrey Hendricks Jr. has an understanding of Jesus that is vastly different than the frightening prosperity gospel writers and preachers of our times. In *The Politics of Jesus* (2006), he writes of Jesus as a revolutionary shaped by his Jewish roots in the exodus story and the political, economic and social factors of living within the Roman Empire. Jesus was all about building a political economy reflective of the kingdom of God—one in which justice reigns person to person, community to community, nation to nation, day by day.

Obrey's working definition of justice is: "doing right by people in society. Moreover, it guarantees people have access to what they need. Justice is egalitarian and grows from love of neighbor." He continues, "To do justice is to make secure the lives of people around you through love, affirmation, and nurturance." Inspired by his parents, Malcolm X, James Cone, Cornel West, and Howard Thurman, Obrey Hendricks Jr. is dedicated to being an intellectual freedom fighter—like all of his mentors and brothers before him.

This prophet packs a punch. He has and will continue to shape prophetic witness for generations to come.

Rev. Dr. Ray Pickett has taken a well-defined, yet significantly different approach to biblical scholarship and justice delivery systems than his colleagues. He did not grow up in the church. He comes to Christianity as convert and through adult baptism. So, he doesn't carry old church baggage. There is a freshness and power to his perspective that always strips away the churchiness of other writers and theologians. He begins and ends in the story of Jesus. Ray is a published and well-respected scholar. But his calling to serve the church grows from his varied secular justice foundation. The texts of Scripture do not lie about injustice and call us to speak truthfully as we battle for justice. Ray has found the model of community organizing to be a worthy method to gather power and make significant change in this world.

As rector at Pacific Lutheran Theological Seminary, Ray has established church-based community organizing as part of the required curriculum. His reason is that pastors will learn about power, organizational strategies, and critical issues facing people who have their backs against the wall. By learning to do "one-on-one" conversations, Ray says, "they will learn how to listen to people's pain because of social injustices they are facing. Our students need to move down from their campus on a hill into the city of Berkeley to offer a more contextually engaged model of theological education. These are challenging times that call for leaders able to mobilize the church to be more engaged in their communities and in the struggle for justice." He teaches the Bible in a way that equips faith leaders to take risks and mobilize their communities to make a difference in the work of social justice.

Ray Pickett does what he says. He is a leader with Genesis, a community organization associated with the Gamaliel National Network in the San Francisco Bay area. He has also developed a national group of Evangelical Lutheran Church of America leaders who are creatively adapting the art of community organizing to engage the local churches and communities around issues of racial equity and social justice.

The world needs forthright biblical scholars and theologians who shape the hearts and minds of faithful religious leaders and laypeople. The five whom I met through this project are true geniuses of justice. They strengthen their students in church, synagogue, college and seminary classrooms, on the streets, and in the academy with integrity and truthful fervor.

Each one lives by the biblical mandate laid out in Micah 6:8: "to do justice, love mercy and walk humbly with God."

## Reflection to Action Questions:

1. The chapter opens with a quote from Abraham Joshua Heschel's *The Prophets*. Reflect on his vision of the prophets. What do you take away

from this powerful description? Does it match your experience with modern-day prophets?

2. Dr. Brueggemann talks about "the Text" of Scripture calling us time and time again to justice action. Look at the Scriptures in this chapter and reflect on how they point toward justice action.

3. Dr. Heschel points out the Bible is interactive. It is God's call to us and our response to God. She asks, "Are we up to the challenge with the Bible? Can we handle it? Can we receive what God has given us?" What do think?

4. In each of the reflections of the five authors, we see vibrant and direct connections between the Bible and our present-day challenges. How do these reflections inspire you to use Scripture for your life of "doing justice"?

# Chapter 3: **Close to You— Generation to Generation**

*Train children in the right way, and when old, they will not stray.*

—Proverbs 22:6, NRSV

Psychologist John Bradshaw once wrote of Jesus:

> Is it any wonder that Jesus of Nazareth turned out to be so well adjusted as he grew from birth, through infancy, through childhood, youth and on into adulthood? At his birth he was called "wonderful, counselor, mighty, king, prince of peace, a child full of grace and truth, savior of the world."

It's true. Jesus of Nazareth was blessed from womb to manger and far beyond. He was beloved from the beginning. He knew love and shared love every day of his life. His nickname was "God is with us!" When everyone close to him beheld him, he saw eyes of love and felt the warm, loving embrace of people who believed in him. His mother sang praises to God about Jesus as he moved in her womb. Held tight at his parents' knees, he was affirmed and celebrated from the moment of birth by angels of God, a host of shepherds, and wandering wise men. Camels, cows, sheep, and goats were there to welcome him. What a crowd of affirmation!

But there was also a shadow side to his arrival, because despotic, narcissistic, sociopathic demagogues are never one-and-done. They keep reappearing in history. Jesus was despised and hunted by King Herod. "God is with Us" was forced to hide in Egypt after being taken through mountains and vast deserts on the journey from Bethlehem to Cairo. From his earliest days, Jesus was made aware of two realities he would face from the actions of love and the reactions of hate. He would be loved and celebrated by those who knew him and hunted by hateful rulers who saw him as a threat to their power.

At the age of twelve, "God with Us"—Immanuel, Joshua, Jesus, Ye-suah (whatever name you choose to call him)—this boy wonder drew crowds of rabbis in Jerusalem's temple who came to garner wisdom from him. But he also intimately knew the shadow of the cross while working at Joseph's side in the carpenter's shop. The angel of the Lord who her-alded his arrival was spot on about this one. So by the age of twelve, Jesus was able to differentiate between good and evil. He was able to refuse and reject evil as a mode of operation. He was able to choose good as the path in his decision-making and actions.

Perhaps every child, given prenatal adoration, and birthed and grow-ing with loving, nurturing, attentive parents and supporters can stand in similar places at an early age. I believe they can. I have seen it happen time and time again. How we encourage, support, nurture, and love our children makes a huge difference. If we look and speak to our children with the same words, spirit, and unconditional love that Jesus saw, heard, and felt during his earliest hours and growing-up days, I believe such love can lead them to be righteous, too.

Mary and Joseph were both courageous. Mary overcame the whispers of disdain and intrigue. Joseph stood his ground on behalf of his adopted son, Jesus. They inspire me. I offer a shout-out to all the moms who speak and embody love and all the dads who embrace all their children—biologi-cal or adopted—and love them just the same, all of them the same.

It takes courage to parent children. Real courage is demonstrated by people who have a lot to lose by standing up and speaking out for what is right and opposing what is wrong. I found a link in my project which con-nected one generation to the next. Courageous and good parenting was clearly passed down to many geniuses of justices. When I asked, "How did you become who you are?" and "who inspired you?" most people spoke of their parents. The positive parental influence of the justice ge-niuses was palpable.

Rev. Dr. Liz Theoharis was born and raised to do justice. It was in her DNA. She remembers interfaith justice meetings happening in her living room and around her kitchen table. She remembered meeting Bishop Des-mond Tutu at her house when she was three years old. Her mother, Nancy Artinian, has been a full-time activist who was politicized during the Viet Nam War. She lived her life following Micah 6:8, "do justice, love kind-ness and walk humbly with God." Liz's father, Dr. Athan Theoharis, was an American historian whose expertise was the Federal Bureau of Investigation,

J. Edgar Hoover, and US intelligence agencies. When he died in July 2021, *The Milwaukee Sentinel Journal* called him "a persistent scourge of the FBI" because he criticized its violations of American civil liberties.

Liz is now co-chair (along with Rev. Dr. William Barber II) of the Poor People's Campaign: A National Call for a Moral Revival. She also directs the Kairos Center for Religions, Rights, and Social Justice at Union Theological Seminary in New York City. She is one of many in this project who claim DNA directed toward justice.

During our first conversation, Ruth Messinger only talked about her mother, Marjorie Weiler. Through fifty-five years at Jewish Theological Seminary, Marjorie and six other Jewish women changed the way the seminary taught and interacted with the world as she directed community relations and communications and advertised in the New York papers and nationwide. Marjorie did ad campaigns about social justice, domestic violence, racism, war, and equality—from the 1950s to the 1970s. She was a pioneer way ahead of her time. For decades, she edited *The Eternal Light*, which was light-years ahead of the times. With Mordecai Kaplan and Abraham Joshua Heschel (whose daughter Susannah is also a genius of justice), Marjorie Weiler left a significant impression on Jewish life and education across many years at JTS.

I believe her greatest gift to this world was her daughter Ruth Weiler Messinger. Ruth has been a central leader in Jewish life and New York politics for more than fifty years. She has passed on the "difference-making" gene to her children and grandchildren—with whom she shares a home in New York City. She organizes people for change and she has fun doing it. With a truthtelling approach and engaging people door-to-door, household to household, Ruth moves people to change systems of injustice, carrying on the work of her mother and passing on the work of the generations upon whose shoulders she stands.

Two pastors who embody the genes in the genius of justice are Rev. Dr. Otis Moss Jr. and his son, Rev. Dr. Otis Moss III. Otis Moss Jr. remembers his grandfather who was born into slavery. His father was a champion of justice in Georgia. A graduate of Morehouse College in 1956 and Morehouse School of Religion/ Interdenominational Theological Center in 1959, Otis Moss Jr. went on to become a leader in the civil rights movement in the 1960s. He is a poet, a musician, a prophet, and a wise man of God. He told me, "I seek to be persistent and outraged, but not so much that rage manages me and anger leaves me bitter." His memories of those who have gone before him—"Mike" King, Fannie Lou Hamer, Vernon Johns, Howard Thurman—all guide his feet and his spirit to be at peace and change the trajectory of injustice in this world. He says, "We must teach the revolutionary content of nonviolence generation to generation. Moreover, each generation has the responsibility of being a prophetic example. We must model this prophetic work for the next generation. If we do it well, they will, too." Otis Moss Jr. has done it well in his family.

Rev. Dr. Otis Moss III reminds me of his father in so many ways. He is poetic, musical, prophetic, and wise. The successful senior pastor of Trinity United Church of Christ in Chicago, Illinois is filled with prophetic imagination. Through preaching, teaching, hip hop, jazz, film, and art, Otis III connects people to the human yearning of justice. He says, "My mother and my father were both deeply committed to ethical and spiritual lives. They were committed to community, justice, and family. In our church, they taught and lived out the transformational belief that we were artists, activists, engineers, doctors, and politicians who were making our neighborhood a brotherhood. That was our guiding principle."

He remembers growing up in the Moss family was a daily tutorial in prophetic witness. "I learned at an early age that poetry and prophetic witness were the same thing. Each call us to pause, reflect, and act. Whether our artistry is written, sung, painted, or performed, it is beautiful and purposeful. When God uses sound, God creates. Poetry in Israel and Chicago is a dynamic aspect of communication. Like poetry, music is found in the space between the notes—not in the notes themselves. I learned this from Thelonious Monk. To that end, justice is God's agape love in public speaking and in human flourishing. God's love is fully human and demands that each of us be fully human, too."

When I asked Otis III what wakes him in the middle of the night he said, "Lack of belief and imagination wake me up. We live in a time when people make deep investments in physical marketplaces. We have entities which run our lives that have no soul. Everything is transactional. When there is a spiritual itch, people scratch it with physical tools. At the heart of it all is collective injustice and acceptance of oppression—a perpetual addiction that never gets fed enough. Too many of us have lost the transcendent in our lives. We lack human imagination and love. We have to find a way out of our addictions. I want fulfillment and joy to be our measures of success."

Liz, Otis Jr., and Otis III are like their parents. Ruth is like her mother. They all reflect that spirit of a young Jesus and other Jewish prophets and rabbis who believed in God and served a greater cause than their own self-satisfaction. I saw this throughout my project. This witness of one generation to the next was woven through the stories of the geniuses of justice. Mothers and fathers, grandmothers and grandfathers, generation to generation nurturing children to be beacons of light and instruments of justice in this world.

Not all of the parents of the geniuses of justice were civic and religious leaders. Some were laborers. Others were lawyers. Some were businessmen and women. A few were pastors or rabbis, but not many. Many were teachers and all placed learning at the heart of raising their children. Some had died tragically when the geniuses were young. Several had parents who battled mental illness. The singular quality that came out of one story after another was love—from at least one parent. They taught them how to love and care for others. And if it wasn't a mother or a father demonstrating and embodying this love, it was another family member whose presence was transformational. Most raised their families with deep connection to faith and action, or at least a conviction for what was "right and wrong." Throughout our conversations, the theme of "see something, say something, do something" was articulated. The fire in the belly of the geniuses often connected to the gut and the DNA of generations from someone in their family. It was rare to find a genius with no parental passion.

As I write, I am fully aware that no matter how much love is shared with our children, some will face physical, social, and mental challenges that keep them from rising and shining. In 2004, I spent time in the Armstrong Barber Shop with James Armstrong, whose story was so beautifully told in the 2012 Oscar-nominated documentary *The Barber of Birmingham: Foot Soldier of the Civil Rights Movement*. On a hot Alabama day, Mr. Armstrong cut my hair in his barbershop and shared many stories with me. He told me about his four children. James was the oldest. Dwight and Floyd integrated the Birmingham public schools as the first Black students in previously all-white schools. His daughter, Denise, was not on the front lines of the civil rights movement. She felt deeply and suffered anguish in the midst of all the white hate and reprisals. Denise was not alone in bearing the pain of her generation. Too many have suffered like her.

Like James Armstrong's children, in each of our families, no matter how much love there is, there are those who are able to step forward and take on the challenges of injustice and those who are affected and afflicted by injustice. Each of them is also gifted in ways that strengthen us. They are part of our story as much as we are a part of theirs.

I think of James Armstrong and his family often. I think particularly of his words about Denise and those who sensitively suffer the wrath of injustice more than others. Generation to generation, we must move with the whole posse that God has given us called "our family." Each family member is a blessing in ways that we may not know or rarely claim. We need to see ourselves bound together with all of them—not just the "geniuses," high-achieving overcomers who we seek to talk about as influencers and inspirations. We are all bound together and justice will prevail only when we name and claim each and every member of our tribe.

Proverbs 22:6 keeps us focused: "Train children in the right way, and when old, they will not stray." May these words inspire you as a parent and a child to find and share "the right way."

## Reflection to Action Questions:

1. There are several remarkable stories about the generational influence of geniuses of justice. Who has shown you and demonstrated in your life what prophetic witness and justice action looks like? A parent? A teacher? How have you responded to this witness in your life?

2. As a parent or adult guide of people in the orbit of your life, how do you teach others and "train children in the right way," to do justice?

3. What are some ways that you see the parents in this chapter passing on the justice gene to their children?

4. Do you know anyone like Denise Armstrong who has suffered from the wrath of injustice? How have they healed those wounds?

# Chapter 4: **Close to Home—My Hometown Family of Justice Warriors**

*I am fain to believe that the time is drawing near when the Christian Church will be able to discern and declare the simple truth that religion is nothing but Friendship, friendship with God and with all people. I have been thinking about it in these last days, and I cannot make anything else, so far as I can see it, this is all there is to it. Religion is Friendship—friendship first with the Great Companion, of whom Jesus told us, is always nearer to us than we are to ourselves, and whose inspiration and help is the greatest fact of human experience. To be in harmony with God's purposes, to be open to his suggestions, to be in conscious fellowship with Him—this is religion on its Godward side. Then, turning to humanity, friendship sums it all up. To be friends with everybody, to fill every human relation with the spirit of friendship, is there anything more than this, that the wisest and best of people can hope to do?*

—Rev. Dr. Washington Gladden

The first time we met, Rev. Dr. Jefferey P. Kee claims it was not "love at first sight." He was suspicious of me. I'm not sure why. He just didn't like me. However, I liked him. I am not sure how that happened. What I am sure about is that almost since our very first time together, "my brother from another mother" and I have been relationally and spiritually inseparable for the past twenty-eight years. Holidays, parties, birthdays, conferences, family gatherings, worshipping together, and sadly preaching one of the eulogies at my father Papa Kee's homegoing, we have been together. We are tethered at the heart of passion for racial and economic justice. We are family. We are friends at the deepest level.

As Washington Gladden writes, religion is nothing more than friendship—with God and other human beings. I love this sentence: "To be friends with everybody, to fill every human relation with the spirit of friendship, is there anything more than this, that the wisest and best of people can hope to do?" Gladden was a genius of justice and so much more. He understood that relationships are at the heart of all real change. I count the friendship I have with this Columbus crew as central to the hope for change and transformation I find in this world.

Fourteen of the fifty-three geniuses of justice have Columbus connections. Some were born and raised here. Others are transplants. They have also been agents of social and faith transformation in my town for many years. They are Dr. Amy Acton, Rev. John Aeschbury, Cantor Jack Chomsky (now retired in Tel Aviv, Israel), Rev. Dan Clark, Rev. John Edgar, Terry Green, Rev. Ben Guess, Minister Adrienne Hood, Lt. Melissa McFadden, Dr. Kee, Rabbi Rick Kellner, Marty Kress, Bishop Lafayette Scales, and Bishop Donald J. Washington. There are even more geniuses of justice in Columbus. In fact, many among each of the men and women named above have told me of two or three more people who they consider geniuses of justice in our community. Columbus is blessed with justice geniuses.

Each of these fourteen geniuses of justice have something special about them. I have written about a number of them in other chapters. Let me lift up the giftedness I have come to know in a few of my Columbus social justice family members.

Columbus has been my home since March 1989. This is where my justice family stands with me and I with them as we approach the challenges of our community. My justice family is courageous. They are justice warriors. The fourteen are part of a much greater family. Truthfully, my justice family has thousands in it. We have marched together, fought together, prayed together, worked together, eaten together, written laws and changed policies together at local and state levels. We have stood strong together for over thirty-three years now. Like our city, my family has grown considerably in the past thirty-three years. Some have joined our ranks because their loved ones have been gunned down in the streets. Others have faced prejudice in their workplaces and have found solidarity and solace in our ranks. We have lost loved ones, too, through transitions to heaven at older ages and some way too young, like Rev. Andrew Foster, Amber Evans, and Reuben Herrera Castillo.

At the heart and soul of my justice family is Rev. Dr. Jefferey P. Kee. He is brilliant, extraordinarily well-read and well-educated, musically gifted, dynamic, energetic, prophetic, poetic, loving, kind, funny, and thoughtful. He is faithful, loving, and just. He is always dressed amazingly and immaculately. He has a way with words that is unmatched among anyone else in our family. He can weave words together in song or in the cause of preaching and justice like no one else.

The Kee family came to Columbus from Birmingham, Alabama. Papa Kee was one of eighteen children and their family faced death-defying racism and inequality. The Birmingham police were notorious for their abuse of Black residents in the city. They beat, arrested, shot, and killed members of the Kee family and so many others. In Jefferey's words, "It was brutal and cruel inequality. It was experiential and not existential. But the love among the eighteen was vast and deep."

Fleeing Birmingham didn't erase violence from Papa Kee's life. When Jefferey was eleven, his older brother was killed by his brother's best friends. No one was ever charged and it remained a cold case forever. One of the long-term effects of this was that Jefferey, now the only son in his family, would never fly together with his father. They always traveled separately to protect the family if anything happened to one or the other while flying. There were other tragedies in the family as well—other young deaths from violence.

All of these losses and his family's deep and abiding faith in God and love for one another and the whole world, kept all of them going through tough times. All of this has developed an undaunted spirit in Jefferey Kee. He organizes people for power all the time. Whether it is predatory lending, incarceration injustice, poverty, crime, refugees in need, or killing unarmed Black men and women on our streets, Jefferey P. Kee keeps his eye on the prize. His gift is relational. He is an interpersonal genius. As he says, "Faith keeps me. I don't keep the faith."

Jefferey's and my greatest work together is Building Responsibility Equality And Dignity (BREAD). We were both founding pastors and have worked shoulder to shoulder in BREAD since 1995. But we have also worked on other projects. Since 2018, we have co-facilitated a group of over seventy-five interfaith clergy called Area Religious Coalition (ARC), working on issues of police reform within the Columbus Division of Police and in the community.

Jefferey brought Lt. Melissa McFadden into my life in the summer of 2018. The tales she told in our first meeting of white Columbus police officers and higher command mistreating Black, brown, and female officers were unbelievable. By that, I mean, it was so bad I didn't believe her. How could white officers treat their own colleagues and fellow officers this egregiously? Moreover, if this was how they treated their colleagues—the thin blue line—as sisters and brothers on the front line of policing, how did they treat the citizens of our community when they were on patrol?

In her memoir, *Walking the Thin Black Line: Confronting Racism in the Columbus Division of Police* (2020), Lt. McFadden tells the truth about her experience. She writes:

> I believe that God is a just God. He is for justice. He does not discriminate. Throughout my career, I have witnessed injustice and discrimination at the hands of many of the same people who believe they are ordained by God to do this work. It is not God's will to mistreat people, even those people who mistreat us. As police officers, we have to rise above vengeance and retaliation to be able to do God's work. In our calling, He shows us the way to bring peace to the land, not create hatred and fear.

> This memoir is my truth. Police officers across the country each have their own truth, which may or may not be similar to mine. Most officers who have witnessed the mistreatment of citizens and fellow officers are unfortunately not free to share their stories; the officers that use their authority in unrighteous ways suppress the truth.

Melissa Weems McFadden grew up in Price Hill, West Virginia, an unincorporated town on the outskirts of Mt. Hope. In her words, "We had a simple, very poor life grounded in family and religion. I was the middle of four sisters, and we fought, well, like sisters." Melissa knew she wanted to be a cop from her earliest days. Raised mostly by her amazing mom, Arlene Weems, who was in Melissa's words, "a mighty woman of God, who raised me to have a strong constitution and a keen sense of justice," Melissa treasured church, education, hard work, and helping people.

Church and her mom instilled in Melissa a strong sense of right and wrong. Honestly, I don't know anyone who has a stronger sense of right and wrong than Melissa. In her words, because of church and her mom, "I have a keen sense of justice. I can't stand injustice, even against people I might not personally like, or who may have harmed me in the past."

The genius of Melissa Weems McFadden is this: she has a deep and clear measure of right and wrong, of justice and injustice, and she tells the truth. In the Columbus Division of Police, as a Black female officer, these qualities have cut against a culture of racism, sexism, discrimination, and lying. The truly amazing thing is that Melissa has survived, endured, and risen through the ranks in such a sick racist culture.

Along with Pastor Kee and over seventy-five other pastors, priests, rabbis, cantors, and imams, Black and white, male and female, we took on the Columbus Division of Police and City Hall. We had "Seven Expectations" that we took to City Hall on September 29, 2018. Four of the expectations called for internal change. Three called for the department to change in relation to our community. All dealt with racism and discrimination from top to bottom. Since then, six of the seven expectations have been met. We are still fighting for one to be completed. We will not surrender. We will not give up or give in.

Melissa McFadden reminds me of Frank Serpico. Serpico was made famous in the movies after he blew the lid of corruption off the New York City police in the late 1960s and early 1970s. Melissa is honest, direct, and unrelenting. She stands with those who are treated poorly by police as she holds her own brothers and sisters in blue to the highest standard. As a lieutenant, she was the highest ranking Black female officer in the Columbus Division of Police until the mayor hired our first Black woman police chief *and* the first person outside our city and ranks to guide the force in the long history of Columbus, Ohio.

Minister Adrienne Hood approached me on a cold January day at a press conference on police violence and the need for accountability to thank me for keeping hope alive. It was I who should have been thanking her. Since her twenty-three-year-old son, Henry Green V, was hunted down on the streets of his neighborhood and executed by a police officer shooting the "kill shot" at close range into his chest, Adrienne has lived every day with the intense grief that all mothers carry in the aftermath of the murderous death of a son. This grief is different because this young man was killed by police officers who are charged with the sworn responsibility to "protect and serve" our community.

The night of June 6, 2016 changed everything for Adrienne and her family as she and they became advocates and activists for justice in our city. She lost her son but she found her voice to cry out on his behalf and on behalf of all the men, women, and children of Columbus and this nation who have been killed by police.

For police, the aftermath of a shooting is often measured by whether it was a "good shooting" or a "bad shooting." In the eyes of the police and too often the courts, almost every police shooting has been deemed "good." In the eyes of justice warriors, like Adrienne and so many others in our town, no police killing of a citizen in our city is ever "good."

Minister Adrienne Hood, of True Love Ministries in Columbus, grew up in Linden. Her childhood was filled with moving a lot. She had a different school every year. In her words, "We were nomads." Her mom struggled to raise three children on her own. But when she secured construction work, the financial worries subsided although the hours were long and the labor was hard. In Adrienne's words, "Life got hard and easy all at the same time." Because of her mother's long hours, beginning at eight years old, Adrienne would take the bus downtown each month with her four-year-old sister to pay the phone, electric, and gas bills.

She grew up early to take responsibilities for her family. Although her father was never there, Adrienne's paternal grandmother, Polly Johnson, was a rock in her life. She said, "Grandma was always there! She was a "four-foot, nine-inch pistol packing piece of fire." She was the matriarch of the family until her ninety-eighth year and her death in early 2021. Thanks be to God for Polly Johnson!

From her earliest years, Adrienne defended the underdog. She would get fired up when children were picking on others. She was always protecting someone else. Her mother taught her not to start fights, but if attacked or defending the defenseless, "Momma told me to give them what they came for when they came."

While we are talking about social justice warriors, Adrienne is an actual warrior, having served twenty years in the US Army. But she doesn't lead with her fists. She leads with a heart of love and hands of prayer and service. She finds her strength in Proverbs 3:5, "My trust is always anchored in God." She believes that God is the champion of the underdog. "God continues to show himself faithful. When we pray, he will answer. Every day, I'm leaning in. I need to remember every day that 'longsuffering' is a fruit of the spirit."

Minister Adrienne Hood is on the front lines of the justice struggles in Columbus. She is an undaunted social justice warrior in her fearless honesty and faith. She finds her strength in the promise God brings in the rainbow in Genesis delivered by God for Noah and the earth. She says, "On the day Bub (Henry) died, a rainbow followed us home. That rainbow caught my attention. Even when the floods come, the flood will not take me out! The rainbow is God's message to me to hold on! So, I look to the heavens for the rainbow's promise of hope."

Rabbi Rick Kellner is senior rabbi of Congregation Beth Tikvah in Worthington, Ohio. He grew up on the south shore of Long Island in Oceanside, New York. Both parents were teachers in the diverse community of Baldwin, New York, which is a community next to Oceanside. Rick's mom taught Spanish and his father was a principal. They brought their children to Baldwin and often brought the teens of Baldwin to Oceanside. Rick grew up accepting and caring for a wide range of people because his parents modeled this kind of life and compassionate presence.

When Rick was six years old, his three-year-old brother was diagnosed with a critical childhood illness. Rick was told not to fight him but to take care of him and protect him. He learned to lead with love as he looked after his little brother, who made it through his early health crises.

Rick credits the cultural literacy of his parents, particularly with Latina heritage, and his brother's early battle for life, as teaching him compassion, love, and care for others. As a Jewish child with a practicing and faithful family growing up post-Holocaust, he also had fears early on of what might happen to him and his parents and family if the world turned on them again. But, these fears, strengthened with his faith, led Rick to a deep and abiding belief in justice. Rick says it this way: "I believed then and believe now, if something is broken, fix it—this includes broken relationships and broken economic systems. Also, if there is something wrong, make it right. If there is someone in pain, ease that pain. Heal that pain. Always recognize people who are seen and treated as 'the other.' Bring people into the core from the edges."

Rabbi Kellner gets angry when he sees selfishness and selfish people who put themselves before everything and everyone else. Quoting the Mishnah, Rick told the story of building a gate in the courtyard. As Rashi says, "we are to be the gate builders. We are the ones who should make doors where there have only been walls before."

Like others in this project, Rick questioned the idea of being called a genius of justice. He said, "All of our great work in Columbus and beyond has been in community and in collaboration with one another—not alone." I reassured my friend that *all* the geniuses of justice work in a collaborative spirit. It is a center piece of their genius—working together and never alone.

Bishop Donald J. Washington and Bishop Lafayette Scales are both born and raised in Columbus. They are truly amazing men of God. Each has dedicated his life to pastoring and caring for a congregation that has grown beautiful, strong, and beloved. Each man is brilliant and gifted in multiple ways—preaching, teaching, music, evangelizing, pastoral care, and nurturing young leaders as they have raised generations of faithful Christians in Columbus, Ohio.

Each one of these amazing geniuses of justice has led his congregation for a very long time. Bishop Washington has led Mt. Hermon Baptist Church for more than forty years. Mt. Hermon has grown exponentially since 1981. Bishop Scales began his work at Rhema Christian Center in 1982 with seven members. In over thirty-nine years his church has grown to thousands and has established six other churches! He has preached across the globe.

Do you know how hard it is to lead a congregation for one year? Now multiply that by seventy-nine-plus years and you get a taste of the power and presence of the Holy Spirit in the lives of these two amazing bishops. God is good!

Bishop Washington is Baptist and Bishop Scales is Pentecostal. They have ascended in service and strength and have been graced with their titles as bishops while shepherding many congregations in their long and fruitful ministry.

Bishop Washington grew up next door to the church he would eventually serve at as senior pastor for forty-plus years—Mt. Hermon Baptist Church. He loved the church and its people and thrived in so many ways growing up. When he went off to war as an Army Ranger, he faced the fiercest fighting of the war—and barely survived combat. He credits his faith with getting him through his near-death experience in war—he "was covered in the blood of Jesus and saved." He rose from the blood of war, covered in the blood of Christ to serve others faithfully and well.

Bishop Scales struggled in the early years of his education in Columbus to succeed in college and beyond. As he says, "I was a kinesthetic learner in schools that understood and nurtured visual, auditory, writing, and reading learners. My teachers didn't know what to do with me. Fortunately, I was nurtured in a church that encouraged me as a kinesthetic learner. Actually—they loved me into being me!"

Bishop Scales is always thoughtful and thorough. He added pages of notes to our conversation. I was moved by the depth of the people and writings that inspired and changed his life. His motivation for justice is saturated and washed completely in the texts of Holy Scripture. He lists Genesis 14:14, Genesis 18:19, and Matthew 1:1 (KJV) as grounding his faithful actions for justice. The Spirit of Cain wakes and moves him to action. Psalm 23, Jesus and Peter, Barnabas, Paul, and Timothy renew and restore his spirit.

He navigates the "shark-infested" water of justice with the following:

- A listening ear
- A patient understanding of systems
- An ability to discover best practices
- A boldness to confront the issues
- An attitude: I don't care who gets the credit
- And—"what does direct action look like in each given context?"

Finally, Bishop Scales is motivated every day to do justice by facing oppression. He knows that oppression is anything that presses people down, anything that limits potential, anything that marginalizes people, anything that does not seek the benefit of all, and anything that steals identity, kills dreams, and destroys destiny. All of this is satanic oppression which is countered by Jesus in John 10:10 and inspires the church in Acts 10:38 to stand up and fight back. And I add, "Amen!"

These men have taught me so much. Through the clarity of the cross, through the depth of their reading and living biblical truths and teachings from the margins—with people who struggle every day to make it in this world—my bishops have become my friends and teachers. They battle systematic racism and live into the prophecy of God to seek fairness and equity for everyone.

I have written about Dr. Amy Acton, Rev. John Aeschbury, Cantor Jack Chomsky, Rev. Dan Clark, Rev. John Edgar, Terry Green, Rev. Ben Guess, and Dr. Marty Kress in other places in this project. All of them live in my locale.

I believe all justice work is local. Whether you are in a large city like Columbus or in a small town, you need to connect with your sisters and brothers who will go to battle with you for the causes of justice for all.

On May 31, 2020, the city of Columbus was on fire in the midst of protests following the murder of George Floyd. Peaceful protests for the multitudes turned into one destructive riot for a few. My church was in the midst of the firestorm that night. I received calls and texts from my brothers and sisters across the city to join me downtown to stand strong in the face of the protests turned destructive. They had my back. That is what family, friends, and social justice warriors do. We have each other's backs. We don't forsake or forget one another. We stand strong together.

When it all comes down to it, religion is friendship. Friendship will keep us together when the powers turn against us. We all know who we are and whose we are. Thanks be to God for my hometown family of social justice warriors.

## Reflection to Action Questions:

1. What do you think of the opening quote that "religion is friendship"? How have you experienced this to be true in your life?

2. Who has your back? Who is standing at your shoulder when your back is against the wall?

3. Who in your town do you admire and wish to join with to do the work of social justice? Have you reached out to them?

4. Reflect on the people in this chapter and consider how they have been drawn into social justice work and movements for change. Do you understand why they have stepped forward? What is pushing you or pulling to act upon injustice in your community? Who are the "hometown social justice warriors" in your life?

# Section 3—**The Inward Journey of Justice**

# Chapter 5: **Cold Anger**

*Hope has two beautiful daughters; their names are Anger and Courage. Anger at the way things are and Courage to see that they do not remain as they are.*

—St. Augustine

ANGER IS USUALLY FRAMED in a negative way. Anger is seen a lack of self-control or the explosive dark side of personal pain. That can be true. What is truer is this: anger is really a sign that something needs to change. That change can be internal or external—or both. But channeling anger for change can strengthen us from inside and out.

In her book *Cold Anger*, Mary Beth Rogers explains that anger gives you energy. Anger that is cold, patient, relational, optimistic, calculated, and hopeful changes the world. "Cold anger is an anger that seethes at the injustices of life and transforms itself into a compassion for those hurt by life. It is an anger rooted in direct experience and held in collective memory. It is the kind of anger than can energize a democracy—because it leads to the first step in changing politics."

Elias Ewing understands "cold anger" even though he did not know it. Elias is a young member of my congregation. When I shared with Elias that I was working on a project on justice, he asked, "Will it be something I can read and understand?" It was great question. I thought I would try out "cold anger" with Elias. I asked him, "Have you ever been in a situation where you were really angry but instead of an outburst, you calmly and coolly focused your anger and did something that made the situation better?" He had been in such a situation. He had been bullied and treated badly. Instead of striking back, he went to teachers and administrators in his school and they addressed the situation and responded appropriately—addressing the injustice and making it better. I said, "That was cold anger!"

Cold anger is an expression used in community organizing. Cold anger takes the fire that surges from the anger we feel at injustice and channels it into action. When used collectively, cold anger amasses power in numbers and focuses the relational power to make change. This power—which is closely related to loving our neighbor—is the ability to organize and act for justice. It is power because it used to make change. It is love because the change that it produces makes people and communities safer, more equitable, more liveable, and more sustainable.

In *Cold Anger,* Mary Beth Rogers tells the story of Mary Moreno. Rogers writes, "For Mary Moreno, that meant learning how to turn her hot anger down a notch or two and make it cold, controlled, and careful, guiding it like some swift, sure missile homing in on its target." Turning anger on a target for developing hope is the best way to transform hot anger into cold anger. Instead of imploding or exploding, you research the topic and problem solve a solution. As in the battle between David and Goliath, you don't need heavy armor and weapons of war to defeat a larger, stronger foe. You need a slingshot and a stone. In other words, you need to use the tools found in prophetic imagination and the power tool kit of the underdog.

The geniuses of justice have often found themselves, like David, with only a stone and a slingshot in the battle against the Goliaths of this world. Through focusing their cold anger, they strategize carefully, organize purposefully, pray constantly, and then when the time is right, bring people together and take their shot.

Rev. John Aeschbury has taught about cold anger as an organizer and now the executive director of the DART organization. He always emphasizes keeping focused on organizing for power. John can be animated and fired up when speaking about injustice and leading the call to action. But this is always tempered with clear objectives and strategies. When colleagues get off track with passionate sidebars, John brings us back into focus. He has his "eyes on the prize" of justice no matter what the issue before us is. The same is true for other organizers with whom I have worked. While some people are seething, they are focusing. While some people might spin with rage, they are fixed on the target and the steps needed to hit the target and achieve victory.

Rev. Dr. Starsky Wilson has laser focus. Now as the chief executive officer of the Children's Defense Fund, Dr. Wilson is focused on changing public policy to care for infants, children, and teens who are so often neglected and forgotten. He will never forget the children. Growing up, both his brother and uncle were murdered on the streets of Dallas, Texas. Starsky knows firsthand what it means to suffer great loss in your own family through gun violence. All three of his sisters were unwed teenage mothers. Starsky knows firsthand what it is like to have "children" birthing and raising children. He grew up with twelve nephews close to his age. Cold anger guides him to stay focused on outcomes and his faith guides him to live into the audacity of hope. When Dr. Wilson chaired the commission investigating the death of Michael Brown in Ferguson, Missouri, it was ice water in his veins and faith in every pore of his body and spirit that led him to bring a just outcome embraced by the community.

There are so many geniuses of justice who have taken the rage that could have buried them in the face of grave injustice and turned the world upside down with cold anger. Look in their eyes and you see passion focused for true and lasting change. How do you go into battle with Goliath? You go with righteous people focused on victory over injustice. You go with one stone and a slingshot. You go with cold anger tempered by courage.

## Reflection to Action Questions:

1. What is your working definition of "cold anger"?

2. Like Elias Ewing, have you ever found yourself in a position to focus your rage as "cold anger"? Once focused and directed, what was the result of your cold anger put toward a transformational work?

3. How have you carefully assessed situations and conditions of injustice and focused your response in a way that has made change happen?

# Chapter 6: **Listen Deeply**

*Listening is much more than allowing another to talk while waiting for a chance to respond. Listening is paying full attention to others and welcoming them into our very beings. The beauty of listening is that, those who are listened to start feeling accepted, start taking their words more seriously and discovering their own true selves. Listening is a form of spiritual hospitality by which you invite strangers to become friends, to get to know their inner selves more fully, and even to dare to be silent with you.*

—Henri J. M. Nouwen

In 1 Samuel 3:1–10, we learn that listening leads to courage and change. In that night we are introduced to one of God's youngest prophets. His name is Shemuel (Samuel), which means "name of God; asked of God; heard by God." God is speaking to this one. He is God's young servant. He is God's young prophet. God calls with purpose and intentionality in the night while "Shemuel" is sleeping. While all are asleep, God calls, "Shemuel, Shemuel . . ." Again, "Shemuel" and again, "Shemuel" and yet again . . . "Shemuel, Shemuel."

After hearing his name spoken by God aloud in the night six times and after all Samuel's running back and forth to Eli, he finally responds as his sage teacher, mentor, and friend tells him to "listen and respond to God." He says to the Lord who is now standing there in front of him, "Speak Lord, for your servant is listening." And so, it begins. Face-to-face, in the dead of night, with the Lord speaking and the prophet listening.

Listening is central in work of justice and in the journey of daily life.

The importance of listening was shared with me by Sr. Margaret Ormond, OP, the first prioress of the Dominican Sisters of Peace and my prioress when I joined the order in 2011 as an associate. I know what you are thinking. How did a Protestant male pastor become a Catholic nun? Good question. When my oldest son heard I was joining the Dominicans, he said, "You are not like other dads. When other dads have a midlife crisis, they leave their families and drive off in a red Corvette. You joined an order of nuns." True.

I didn't know I was having a midlife crisis. I thought I was listening to God. I thought I was following the initiative of the Holy Spirit. I listened to the Holy Spirit calling me to join with this new order which brought together eight different streams of "the Order of Preachers." I wanted to be part of the unity of the church. I became an associate in 2011 and I have been blessed by the Dominican charism of preaching with holy fire ever since.

Sr. Margaret has been my inspiration for a long time. We first met in Rome in 2004. Her welcome to my family on a hot summer day at the Dominican headquarters and Santa Sabina Church will forever be in my heart.

In June 2021, she finished her term as the president of the Dominican Academy, an all-honors, college prep high school for girls in New York City. Besides being the first prioress of the Congregation of Dominican Sisters of Peace, she is well-known throughout the Dominican Order as a result of her cross-cultural ministerial experience.

Before becoming the Dominican Sisters of Peace's first prioress in 2009, Sr. Margaret ministered for the Porticus Foundation as a consultant on Leadership Among African Religious, advocating on behalf of women in many areas of the continent. Previously, Sr. Margaret served as international coordinator of Dominican Sisters International for nine years. For over ten years, she facilitated Dominican congresses in the Philippines, El Salvador, South Africa, Kenya, Peru, and Hungary, and traveled to many countries to speak on such topics as religious life in this century and the global realities faced by the Church. In 1986, Sr. Margaret was asked to serve as co-director of Parable, a national organization for the promotion of Dominican life and mission.

She has had many honors and served across the nation and the world spreading the good news of the gospel of Jesus Christ and sharing his love with all.

Sr. Margaret is a genius of justice. As we talked, she said the word *listen* at least twenty times. Throughout her ministry, she has listened deeply to women, men, teens, and children. It started when she was child in Brooklyn, New York. She was the fifth of six children who were born over seven and one-half years. She spent a lot of time listening to her older siblings and parents. Her family was not only close in age, but close in every imaginable way.

When the time came for her to head out into the world, it was a huge transition. She went from an all-girls Dominican Academy to an all-women Marymount College to her first assignment as a teacher in the co-educational setting at Steubenville Central Catholic High School in Steubenville, Ohio. She grew up fast in Steubenville and it was there that she fell in love with teaching. She still goes back to the reunions for the classes she nurtured and taught many years ago!

She said, "When you listen deeply, you receive such a blessing. You gather information, you discover the spirituality of the person, you hear what makes them curious and creative, and you hear simple and honest answers to the stories of people's lives."

Listening deeply has been the gift she has brought to Dominicans worldwide. She says, "When I listen, I am inspired by the good in people. They point me to a better way. By asking questions and acknowledging the good within them and the good which they have done, God widens the space of grace."

Sr. Margaret added, "I always try to bring prayer to the atmosphere. I know we all share something in common as sisters. We are all called to preach and live good news about Jesus Christ." She continued,

> Our life in the Spirit of God is really simple. It is about preaching, holiness, and joy. We are called to bring out the best in others. That is what preaching does. We are also called to see the holiness in others. And we believe everyone is capable of holiness. Finally, we are called to do it all with joy! We have to be inspired by young women and men who have their lives in front of them. Pay attention to their alertness. Draw them into conversations and draw them out of their sadness and loneliness. No one should sit alone in this world. We are called to connect and listen. It is listening that leads to justice.

Sr. Margaret offers us all a priceless jewel in her gift of listening deeply. It is a jewel for life and living. It is also a jewel for justice. Like you, the most profound moments in my life have come while deeply listening to someone. Absorbing their wisdom and pain, growing from their insights and struggles, listening to their lives, I have been changed.

Listening is a gift.

It is a gift like the gifts of Epiphany in the Christian experience which are laid before us each year by the wise ones in our lives. No, I do not mean gold, frankincense, and myrrh. I am speaking of three gifts: "courage to change," "overcoming acedia," and "humility to bind the broken."

Consider first the gift of the courage to change. Not one of us dropped from the sky. Each of us has a story that needs to be heard. Our stories carry joy and celebrations as well as struggles and pain. In a sense, your life itself is a story of many epiphanies, many points of light, life, and love all connected by a God who has stayed by your side through the struggles and the joys of your life. You needed courage to change, to simply get up this morning. You are a gift from God to many more people than you imagine, people whose lives you have touched and healed.

The courage to change can be elusive. There are those, like Maya Angelou, who have literally lost their voices sometime in their lives. When, as a young woman, Maya found her poetic voice again, the caged bird that was within her sang freely of hope and God's grace. Maya Angelou became our nation's poet laureate. She wrote, "I can be changed by what happens to me. But I refuse to be reduced by it." And also, "If you don't like something, change it. If you can't change it, change your attitude."

From Sr. Margaret, I was reminded once again to never be reduced by all that has happened in your life. Be changed by it. And remember that your attitude, fired in the furnace of gratitude, can always be changed to face any demons—past, present, or future.

May God grant you the courage to change.

Second, consider the gift of overcoming acedia. The fathers of the early church went to the desert to pray and to battle the devil. Some thought they went to escape the challenges of daily living in the metropolis. They went because, like their savior Jesus Christ, they felt they could confront the devil and overcome his horrible destructiveness. It was a noble experiment. But, often besetting the desert fathers was "acedia" or "the devil of the noonday sun." Acedia is spiritual boredom, indifference to matters of prayer and faith, and simple laziness.

Acedia didn't die in the desert with the church fathers. Acedia still resides in the hearts and minds of all too many people, too many pastors, priests, nuns, rabbis, and imams today. It manifests itself in a refusal to embrace spiritual growth. The sins of acedia still appear today. People lose their passion for serving. They feel overwhelmed by the challenges of their lives. They give in and give up. They become apathetic, lazy, and bored too easily. They stop reading books. They stop listening to God and to other people. They don't pray with regularity and discipline. They speak without carefully thinking and praying through scriptural texts (and iPhone texts) and dismiss all the trouble of preparing before preaching. Acedia—rather than the Holy Spirit—holds them in its devilish noonday grip.

You must fight back and overcome acedia in your life. Don't prop yourself in front of screens instead of praying and reading and learning and living. Be with people in their need and care for them there. But take care of yourself as well. If you don't listen to the Spirit of God, acedia will overcome you.

The apostle Paul was a man on fire for God. Fueled by the power of the Holy Spirit, he was alive at noonday—and all the other times of the day and night! In his passion he spoke about everything and got some things all wrong. That's why everyone has opinions about Paul and disagrees or is outraged by him in some way or another. But Paul's power to push our buttons also means he was on fire when he wrote his words. We all know that fire can burn or warm. It can fuel hope or destroy indiscriminately.

Let us not get stuck in the dust of the noonday devil. Rather, let us hear Paul's words in Ephesians. Let us gain access to God with boldness and confidence through faith in him who called us to be teachers and preachers of God's holy word—even Jesus Christ our Lord. I see in Sr. Margaret one who seeks in her own life to overcome acedia and become an even greater more passionate lover and liver of God's holy Word.

Finally, think of the gift of humility to bind the broken. In John 13, Jesus kneels to wash his disciples' feet. Judas already has it in his heart to betray Jesus. Jesus knows his crucifixion is coming soon. Yet there he is—on the floor with a basin of water, washing their feet, even over the incessant protests of Peter. Jesus says, "You call me Lord and teacher. Then do as I have done!" Be servants to all.

In his short story "The Ragman," author Walter Wangerin tells the mythic story of a man who walks the streets meeting people in their pain—modeling Christ in the city. I take poetic and prophetic license in relation to gender identity. Let's allow Walter's "Rag Man" to be the "Rag Woman." In the spirit of Sr. Margaret, all Dominican Sisters of Peace worldwide, and all women of all faiths and no faith at all, I share the story to honor their lifetime of love binding the broken across the globe.

One Friday morning, a rag woman appears on the streets of her city as a strong healthy woman with a cart filled with clean rags. She moves through the city and meets torn, tattered, and broken people on the streets of her city. As she encounters them, she picks up the rags and tattered pieces of their tattered and torn lives and heals them—one by one—as she wraps them with her clean cloth. There is the little girl crying and left alone after being beaten by her parents. There is the man homeless and huddled in a corner crying in loneliness. There is the man with one arm who cannot work because he cannot carry the weight of the world.

As the clean cloth touches the lives and skin of the wounded ones, the rag woman carries away all the bloodied and torn rags. She carries them—like the sins of the world—to the city dump. There, having taken on the pain of the world and having healed the wounded, the worn, and broken of heart, mind, and body, the rag woman lies down on the pile of rags, exhausted and overcome by the pain of the world, and dies that Friday night as the sun sets.

But this story doesn't end with Friday's death. It ends in resurrection joy. As the narrator draws the story to a close, he says:

But, then, on Sunday morning, I was wakened by a violence. Light—pure, hard, demanding light—slammed against my sour face, and I blinked, and I looked, and I saw the last and the first wonder of all. There was she was—the rag woman, folding the blanket most carefully, a scar on her forehead, but alive! And, besides that, healthy! There was no sign of sorrow nor of age, and all the rags that she had gathered shined for cleanliness.

Well, then I lowered my head and trembling for all that I had seen, I myself walked up to the rag woman. I told her my name with shame, for I was a sorry figure next to her. Then I took off all my clothes in that place, and I said to her with dear yearning in my voice: "Dress me." She dressed me. My Lord, she put new rags on me, and I am now a wonder beside her. The rag woman. The Christ.

Listening deeply leads to the epiphanies of our lives. Listening deeply leads us to these three gifts of the magi:

"The Courage to change"

"Overcoming acedia"

"Humility to bind the broken"

Sr. Ormond has all of these gifts. She is a true genius of justice. She will always be my prioress and friend. She has listened deeply throughout her life. Through her listening, she has manifested the light, life, and love of God.

May you listen deeply. God is standing before you calling you by name. And there is only one reply. It is the reply from the lips of "Shemuel" long ago. "Speak Lord, your servant is listening."

## Reflection to Action Questions:

1. Take a look at the opening quote from Henri J. M. Nouwen. How do approach listening as a sacred act?

2. Sr. Margaret Ormond has dedicated her life to listening deeply to God and to others. She offers many examples of doing this. How have you paused, taken a deep breath, and listened deeply to God and other people? What difference have you seen when listening preceded speaking? When have you asked questions before making statements about conditions of injustice?

3. I name three gifts that add to the depth of listening. First, the courage to change. Second, overcoming acedia in your life. Third, having the humility to bind the broken. How have these three gifts been manifested in your life? If they haven't been, how could you dedicate yourself to channel these gifts for change?

# Chapter 7: **Pray and Mean It**

*For surely, I know the plans I have for you, says the Lord, plans for your welfare and not for harm, to give you a future with hope. Then when you call upon me and come and pray to me, I will hear you.*

—JEREMIAH 29:11–12

THROUGHOUT MY LIFE I have witnessed the power of prayer. I have felt God's hand while praying on my knees. I have witnessed God's saving and healing grace when praying with those in need. I have witnessed doors open, hearts change, minds move from evil to good, policies shift from harmful to helpful when prayers are lifted to God. When we pray and mean it, great things happen.

Prayer matters. Prayer certainly matters to geniuses of justice, many of whom have spent their life in prayer. Before and during marches, in public witnesses, in meeting with mayors, governors, and presidents, and where two of three of them gather to plan and simply to be with one another, their prayers to God shape and form each of their conversations. I have witnessed prayer as a glue that holds us together like the blasting shofar that calls us to do the right thing for our sisters and brothers in need of justice and peace.

For Christians, the Lord's Prayer is believed to be "the perfect prayer." Dr. John Perkins, now ninety-two years old, prays continuously each day of his life. However, it is the Lord's Prayer that centers all his faith and action. He says, "The Lord's Prayer is our daily call to daily action for justice. I will be in church sometimes listening to the Lord's Prayer and I give thanks to God that he gave us the prayer that frames our care for the hungry poor and our love for all humanity."

Presented in the Gospels in Luke 11:2–4 and Matthew 6:9–12, the Lord's Prayer is a call for the coming of the kingdom of God's justice on earth. We know it in its liturgical form, which is often spoken in worship like this:

> Our Father who are art in heaven, hallowed be thy name,
>
> thy kingdom come; thy will be done on earth as it is in heaven.
>
> Give us this day our daily bread.
>
> And forgive us our debts as we forgive our debtors.
>
> And lead us not into temptation but
>
> deliver us from evil,
>
> for thine is the kingdom and the power and the glory forever. Amen.

There is such richness to this prayer. ". . . Give us this day our daily bread . . ." How simple. Jesus knew how to keep things simple. He knew that finding something to eat was a serious problem that literally consumed and still consumes much of the daily energy of most of the world's population. Jesus knew that without bread and water in your belly, the rest of this message makes no sense. It will never reach you. Without bread, you become distracted and disoriented. Without bread, your energy is depleted and your body breaks down. Basic human needs must be met for the kingdom to become real. Daily bread is essential for life, breath, and daily existence. Beyond simple existence, Jesus knew that eating together was a sign of God's love and justice. He knew that bread broken and shared was the greatest communion with God and humanity, linking heaven and earth.

He also knew that the lack of daily bread was a reflection of greed and neglect on the part of those who "have" resources and not laziness on the part of those who "have not." So, when the hungry poor pray for daily bread, it is out of immediate need. When those who have food pray, it becomes a commitment not to merely find food for yourself, but to provide bread for the world. Our prayer becomes a prayer for justice, not merely for our next meal.

"Give us this day our daily bread" must cause each of us to reflect on our core values. In a hungry world, how have I provided food for another one of God's children this day? If we ignore or spiritualize Jesus' command outside of his prayer to "feed my sheep," then we become the shepherds that the prophet Ezekiel warned of in Ezekiel 34:3–4: "You eat the curds, clothe yourselves with the wool and slaughter choice animals, but you do not take care of the flock. You have not strengthened the weak, healed the sick, or bound up the injured." By doing this, we care for ourselves and let the rest of the world suffer.

Think of this another way. If we were to shrink the world's population to a village of a hundred people with all the ratios remaining the same, there would be fifty-nine Asians, fifteen Europeans, nine Central and South Americans, eleven Africans, five citizens of the United States, and one from Canada. There would be fifty-two females and forty-eight males. Thirty people would be white, seventy people would be of other races. Thirty people would be Christian and seventy would be of other religions. Thirty would be able to read and seventy would be illiterate. Although we in the United States represent only five people in this global village, we possess 59 percent of the village's wealth. Our 5 percent uses 54 percent of the village's expendable resources, including food. Put yourself in the place of the other ninety-five villagers. As we Americans own so much and consume so much of the village's resources, is it any wonder that the other ninety-five villagers feel jealous, defensive, hateful, and resentful of the way we relate to them?

It is time to live the kingdom values of Jesus. When he said, "For those to whom much has been given, much is expected in return," he was speaking to us. I recommend we get out of our comfortable five homes in the village of this world and visit the other ninety-five villagers. Do you see how this prayer works? It does not invite us to close our eyes and pray in private. It compels us to get up off our knees and open our eyes to the other ninety-five global villagers who need bread today. Some of them are knocking at our doors. Most of them are too weak to stand. All of them need bread today.

Ironically, this clause of the prayer is different in Matthew and Luke's versions. The Greek is tricky, but Matthew seems to mean, "Give us today our bread for tomorrow." Luke clearly means, "Give us each day our daily bread." While scholars tangle about the spiritual meaning of "bread for tomorrow" versus "bread for here and now," I move on with this thought: perhaps each writer had it right. Prayers for tomorrow's bread are only possible when we have eaten today. Prayers for reconciling heaven and earth through the breaking of bread are, in the end, the true meaning of Jesus' reconciling words. In essence, he is saying, "Feed my people here and now, and I will feast with you at the banquet table in heaven."

The Lord's Prayer dives deeper into the relationships between us and among us than its focus on daily bread. Forgiveness, temptation, evil, and living fully the values of God's kingdom on earth call the one who prays deeper into relationship with God and our sisters and brothers on earth.

Prayer can be many things—but let us focus here on how it calls us to justice action with and for God and humanity. Prayer is an essential tool to enable us to connect life and justice in ways that will not fail even when challenged, sometimes brutally.

As a Christian pastor and one who prays to and often through Jesus, I find that prayer forms in the Christian part of my family are very incarnational. They have a close relationship between the real and present reality of Jesus and each individual who prays in his name. It is very personal.

When I step outside my Christian prayer circle, I am moved by my family of faith that prays to our One God in different ways, with different voices. The prayers of the faithful from the world's religions, empower all our action for justice and peace. My friends' prayer forms and languages speak to God in varied and beautiful ways. It is all our prayers together that connect all of us in our work for justice. Prayer really matters.

Cantor Jack Chomsky is a genius of justice who believes in and practices his faith prayerfully. For thirty-eight years, the cantor emeritus of Congregation Tifereth Israel in Columbus, Ohio, tuned his voice and heart to prayer. As an observant Jew, prayer is part and parcel of everyday life. Prayer is present in daily thought and action in this model of living a Jewish life like blood coursing through the body.

When Jack and I talked about justice, the conversation led to a focus on prayer. Spirituality and justice are bound together. There is no separating one from the other. While many focus on the seasons and high holy day markers that carry Jewish life forward in faith, Jack suggests that the foundation for our being able to focus consistently on justice comes through daily prayer and daily commitment and experience, so that it becomes part of how we see, hear, and feel everything.

Jack said a typical concern expressed by contemporary Jews is that "the old-fashioned prayers have no meaning for me" or that often "I only feel God's presence when I'm in a special place in nature." (This also sounds familiar to me as a Christian pastor.)

Jack discovered that incorporating traditional prayer habits, wrestling with the meanings of words and being unafraid to confront ideas that make us uncomfortable, frees us to find that which we *do* connect with—and to develop habits that lead us to a "joy and justice focus." He continues, "In the morning service alone, there are at least a hundred different phrases that focus you on what you ought to do today. The morning prayer takes us through history, ideas, emotions that carry a person through the whole day. The prayer is telling us to look at the world with our eyes open."

In "working on prayer" and teaching and leading, Cantor Chomsky established the phrase/concept "pray and mean it." He doesn't claim to have invented the phrase—but keeping it as a refrain that comes up in many of his efforts has been helpful.

"Many people complain that the prayers are meaningless," he notes. "I would say that 'true' or effective prayer can't be meaningless. If it's meaningless, the pray-er hasn't found the practice or words that activate spirit, heart, and mind. Everyone really needs to find their own path—but within the Jewish world, we do have a very deeply defined existing path. Rather than trying to create a new one—let's find out which elements of these path are treasures of and for the soul."

Recently, Jack wrote to me these important thoughts on Jewish prayer and the connection between prayer and justice.

> One important element of traditional Jewish prayer is that one needn't look for what to say. Our prayers are a fixed liturgy. This distinguishes Jewish practice from both Christian and Muslim practices, albeit in different ways. Jewish prayer tradition is three times a day—short in the evening, long in the morning, shortest in the afternoon. At the core of all three of those experiences is the Amidah—the central (standing—which is what Amidah means) prayer that has nine blessings (except on Shabbat when it's reduced to seven). The evening and morning prayers also include the Sh'ma—which acknowledges God's uniqueness and relationship to the Jewish people and vice versa, and serves as a reminder of what we're supposed to do—and the Sh'ma says unequivocally that there is reward or punishment based on performance.

Jack said,

> As an adolescent this turned me off, because it clearly wasn't the way of the world. It was a long time until I understood the power of aspirational concept even when we are experiencing the opposite. "I have described the *morning* experience (daily and Shabbat) as simply ME/YOU/US/US. This is a summary of the trajectory of our daily prayers—which begin with a ME section [in Hebrew, this section is called Birkot Hashachar—morning blessings], noticing that we are alive and we are our unique selves. Lest we get too impressed with those selves, we immediately get to the YOU

section [in Hebrew, this section is P'sukei D'zimrah—passages of song], a series of psalms and other recitations reminding us many times and many different ways of the greatness of the Creator.

That brings us to the 'two USes'—which would be the Sh'ma and the Amidah. The first US is a declaration that, in this world in which we are *so* blessed, and there is so much that God has done, *we* are in relation to that God. God is one—God is our God. We belong to God. And God says 'this is what you're supposed to do' and if you do it, things will be great and if you don't, things will be the opposite of great. And *then*, we get to the second US, which is the moment we take three steps forward into God's presence and recite the things that are in our heart and on our mind—things we worry about, things we want help with.

Jack concludes, "Those two USes are pretty radical statements—especially if we haven't prepared for them. By the nature of public prayer, most people arrive in synagogue after we've done the ME/YOU sections—and possibly even after we've done one or both of the US sections. No wonder they are unmoved by prayer!"

The foundation of Jewish prayer culture is to develop excellent thankfulness practices. The practice of becoming joyfully thankful individuals who are part of a community engaged in the same thing puts us on a potentially powerful spiritual and justice path.

Jack continued on the relationship to prayer connecting to justice.

Prayer helps us to pay attention. It is stunning how much justice comes up in the composed prayers of the rabbis and in the psalms—and in everything. One thing to keep in mind is that different people will interpret justice and God's intention in different ways. So, although you and I may believe that God directs us to pursue justice that lifts up the poor and confronts the powerful, others—whether Jews, Christians, or adherents of other religions—may be inspired by the same verses to pursue policies directly opposed to those we're fighting for.

Generally, it appears to the world that people who really, really believe deeply in GOD and GOD'S WILL seem to be fundamentalists, right-wingers, anti-abortion, pro-gun. (What's up with that?!) I advocate a rich religious life that helps give me the strength to deal with the struggle—and helps me strengthen those around me. I feel like I'm redeeming God's good name and real intention—intention that seems so clear to me by the themes and vocabulary

I encounter over and over and over in prayer and Tanach (this is the Hebrew word referring to the Bible—an acronym of Torah, N'viim, and K'tuvim—Torah, Prophets, and Writings).

Jewish daily prayers speak about the world as God creates it and as it is meant to be. God is compassionate for the earth and all who God creates, emancipates, and rescues. Adonai brings redemption when we call upon the name of God. People name and express awareness of God's goodness, sing in exaltation of God's justice, and celebrate Adonai's grace and colossal kindness. Meanwhile, God establishes justice for the downtrodden, provides bread for the hungry, reinstates those shackled away, gives sight to the blind, straightens up those bowed down, adores the righteous, protects strangers, raises orphan and widow, and straightens the path of the wicked.

Jack resumes, "That's just the *first* part of the "YOU" section. There is *so* little in prayer that is negative—although it *is* there and it *must* be there. Between the Sh'ma and the Amidah (the two US sections) are passages that affirm the liberation of our people from Egypt—how God performed miracle after miracle after miracle for us."

> So, when I go through the liturgy and I see that God did this and this and this and that and that and this and that . . . I'm marching toward freedom—from slavery in history—but toward freedom in our time for all who need it—including me, but not just me. The Amidah's nineteen blessings cover a range of issues: history, nature (including resurrection . . . but that means something very different in my world), holiness, wisdom, repentance, forgiveness, redemption, healing, agricultural and economic success, bringing us together, bringing simple justice, fighting our enemies, blessing the righteous, Jerusalem, redemption, *hearing* us, accepting our offering, thanksgiving, peace. You will notice there is one negative idea there—"fighting our enemies." Sometimes we need it—like after terrorists murder dozens of people. Having it there helps us to acknowledge that we need it without being given over to it entirely.

Cantor Jack Chomsky is a genius of justice grounded in prayer. He was the key leader in the Jewish community in Columbus building connections between Jews and everyone else. He did this prayerfully, thoughtfully, and purposefully. The bridges he built for thirty-eight years between Jews, Christians, Muslims, Buddhists, and every other faith expression in our city made a world of difference. He also built bridges across the world—always leading while he prayed and praying while he led.

Jack Chomsky is one of many geniuses of justice who lift up the heart of prayer as the center of his or her faith in action. Fr. Dan Noll, Rev. Charles Heyward, Fr. Phil Egitto, Minister Adrienne Hood, Pastor Shane Claiborne, Bishop Donald J. Washington, Rabbi Rachel Timoner, Sr. Simone Campbell, and Congressman Rev. Bobby Rush all specifically lifted up the power of prayer and worship in their lives. Most of the geniuses acknowledged they would be nowhere and nothing without prayer and the presence of God in their lives.

Fr. Dan Noll, pastor of Mary Queen of the Holy Rosary Parish in Lexington, Kentucky spoke of the centrality of prayer in his daily life. He grew up on a small farm in a "German Roman Catholic ghetto" in rural northern Kentucky. In his words, "We had no diversity in my community growing up." They had the close-knit community of an isolated and segregated group of people (which is the definition of a ghetto). And there prayer was the center of daily life and worship. Fr. Dan remembers, "I wanted to be true, honest, and authentic. I wanted to be a person of integrity. I believed in the communion of saints and I couldn't be in touch with the saints without being in touch with justice." From his early years, he developed a devotion to prayer in the Psalms and the daily office. Reading the Scripture from the margins and experiencing the fullness of faith in prayer and action guide his daily steps.

Rev. Charles Heyward has found that prayer and worship inform everything he does every day. In twenty years at St. James Presbyterian Church, on James Island, South Carolina, it was the prayer and worship life of the congregation that strengthened and became the backbone of everything the congregation did.

Fr. Phil Egitto, pastor of Our Lady of Lourdes Catholic Church in Dayton Beach, Florida, finds his inspiration from people of prayer—including Sr. Simone Campbell, Fr. Richard Rohr, Sr. Joan Chittister, and St. Francis of Assisi. "Prayer connects my congregation and me with 'God under the bridges,'" Fr. Phil says. "We find ourselves not telling God what to do, but listening and responding to the real presence of Christ in the homeless poor." He continues, "I don't pray prayers to a 'magic Jesus' but the real presence of Christ in this world and in the people God calls us to serve."

Minister Adrienne Hood, at True Love Ministries in Columbus, Ohio, finds solace in prayer. She attributes Proverbs 3:5 to strengthening her in her daily walk of faith—"trust always anchored in God!" She says,

"I am leaning into the Lord every day and he continues to show himself faithful every day!"

Pastor Shane Claiborne has dedicated his life to "common prayer." As pastor in the Simple Way Community in Philadelphia, Shane wrote *Common Prayer: A Liturgy for Ordinary Radicals* (2010), along with Jonathan Wilson-Hartgrove and Enuma Okoro. The prayer book was designed to help individuals, families, and congregations pray together across denominations. This little book of common prayer calls people together each day with the same songs, Scriptures, and prayers. *Common Prayer* is a tapestry of prayer that intends to help the church be one as God is one. This universal prayer book allows readers to greet each day together, remembering significant dates and heroes across many faith traditions as well as important historic dates in the struggle for freedom and justice. *Common Prayer* has morning prayers for each day of the year, evening prayers for each of the seven days of the week, a midday prayer to be repeated throughout the year, and prayers for special occasions. In addition, there are morning prayers for Holy Week. *Common Prayer* also includes a unique songbook composed of music and classic lyrics to more than fifty songs from various traditions, including African spirituals, traditional hymns, Mennonite gathering songs, and Taizé chants. Pastor Claiborne has not only written a book about prayer and with prayers, but prayer is the essential center of his life that guides all his steps of daily life and justice action.

Bishop Donald J. Washington of Mt. Hermon Baptist Church in Columbus, Ohio places prayer at the center of his life. He rises early each morning and begins each day with the study of Scripture and prayer. He journals every day. He places his complete trust in God for deliverance. He finds strength in Judges 31 and the story of God delivering Israel in spite of all the wrongs done. "Like Israel in Judges 31, I believe our God saves us in spite of ourselves," Bishop Washington says.

Rabbi Rachel Timoner found her way back to Judaism through Buddhist teachings and mystical experiences. "Spirituality is really big in my life," she told me. "It is my daily prayer and expression of prayer in my Jewish tradition that grounds me in everything I do." In 2010, Timoner's *Breath of Life: God as Spirit in Judaism*, uncovered the role of God as Spirit in Jewish sacred texts. She reveals the origins of Jewish spirituality and the Christian Holy Spirit with her engaging voice that compels Christians and Jews to take a look at the Spirit of God.

Sr. Simone Campbell, like Rabbi Timoner, has been influenced by Buddhist meditation and mystical teachings as well as Jewish and Christian mystics. She begins each day in prayer. Her life is led and guided by prayer. Her community, the Sisters of Social Service, have a discipline of prayer that has also empowered and encouraged her through the years. The mass and the prayers and presence of Christ in the Eucharist guide her daily faith as well.

Congressman Rev. Dr. Bobby Rush is pastor of Beloved Community Church of God in Christ, Chicago, Illinois. He says the most important work of his life is in this congregation, even though he has served as Illinois' First US Congressional District representative since 1993. He continues, "In the prayers and worship of the people of God, I have come to know the fullness of God's love. When we pray, we are called, in the words of William Wilberforce, to 'take what is unfamiliar and make familiar for Christ.'"

Prayer is found at the heart and soul of all the geniuses of justice. Although he is now praying half a world away in Tel Aviv, Israel, I can still hear the voice of my cantor and my friend Jack Chomsky praying and meaning it. Praying and praising God has led billions of people through thousands of years to find hope in the midst of tough times. Justice is rooted in the scriptural texts, the hymns and tunes of faith, and in the prayers of the people.

We are reminded in Jeremiah 29:11–12 that God has plans for each of us. God's plans are for our welfare, not our harm. They are for a future with hope. All God is calling us to do is come to God and pray to God. That is simple and clear.

My prayer to God is that we may all pray and mean it.


## Reflection to Action Questions:

1. I have so many questions for you about your life of prayer:

    Most important, do you pray and mean it?

    What moves you pray in the first place?

    How do you pray?

    To whom do you pray?

    For what and for whom do you pray?

    Are you speaking or singing and listening in prayer?

    Are you ever silent in prayer?

How does injustice drive you to prayer?

How does your work for justice bring you to your knees?

2. Cantor Jack Chomsky does a deep dive into Jewish daily prayer. As you read his reflections, how does it change your approach to prayer?

3. There a number of stories about geniuses of justice as people of prayer. Which ones touch you and help you in your life of prayer?

4. Write your own prayer for justice here:

# Chapter 8: **Open the Gates**

*Open to me the gates of righteousness; I shall enter through them;*
*I shall give thanks to the Lord. This is the gate of the Lord; The*
*righteous will enter through it.*

—PSALM 118:19–20

EACH ONE OF US looks at our life and asks questions. We think about the roads we have traveled. Did we make the right choices? Did we honor the fullness of God's call in our life? We wonder if we have achieved what we set out to do. We ponder if we truly responded to the whisper of God at midnight. Were we honest enough? Faithful enough? Good enough?

There were four women of faith who touched me deeply in this project. Each has spent her life opening the gates of righteousness and justice for all God's children. Each has come to her calling in different ways. These women will fill you with hope as you ponder questions about your own choices to support and help others. One is a rabbi, one is a bishop, one is a Catholic nun, and one is a pastor and a mercy and justice coordinator. Rabbi Rachel Timoner, Bishop Yvette Flunder, Sr. Simone Campbell, SSS, and Rev. Sarah Marsh stand at the gates of righteousness every day and make a way for women, men, and children where there seems to be no way.

What inspires me about each woman is tremendous depth of prayer and reflection, compassionate organizing for action, and the gift for preaching and teaching. Each woman is different but they all embrace love in a collaborative action in the daily fight for justice.

As a freshman at Yale University, Rabbi Rachel Timoner looked out her window at Pierson College one night, seeing the gates of Yale. On her side of the gates were the hallowed grounds of the exclusive Ivy League university. On the other side were the streets of New Haven, Connecticut. Inside the gates, wealth and comfort reigned. On the other side of the gates, the homeless poor slept in cardboard boxes. Inside the gates, the students were well fed and well educated. On the other side of the gates, parents struggled to feed their hungry children and get them to school each day. Inside the gates, the world was as it should be. On the other side of the gates, the world was not as it should be.

That night, Rachel decided to commit her life to those who lived on the other side of the gates. She started organizing students to serve at a soup kitchen and care for her neighbors in need. She organized the Yale/New Haven Alliance, which addressed a glaring and critical issue. Yale University paid no taxes to the city of New Haven. She was part of an economically unjust practice and she couldn't accept that. Through her efforts, Yale "found" $10.4 million that was on the books as a surplus. The people of the other side of gates would be served by the wealthy ones on her side of the gates.

In her early days at Yale, Rachel described herself as a "cultural Jew." She had given up practicing her faith. Today, Rabbi Rachel Timoner is the senior rabbi of Congregation Beth Elohim in Brooklyn, New York. She is still organizing her congregation and community to bring justice to this world.

Rachel still asks the question that informed her life so many years earlier at Yale, "Did I open the gates?"

Rabbi Timoner has spent her life loving people and pushing the gates open to all. She is not the only genius of justice who opens the gates, although she is really good at making this world a better place. She does so through prayer, education, worship, love and direct action. She opens the gates through her prayers, her spirituality, her writings, and the way she organizes her synagogue life.

From her early days at Yale, Rachel Timoner has been an organizer but in those days her faith was not fully formed. She organized the Yale/New Haven Alliance. Then she went on to organize for justice in San Francisco. She organized with women and with LGBTQ youth. Her passion for justice drove her. But something was missing.

She found herself up at night thinking about God. She was inspired by the writings of Buddhist peace activist Thich Nhat Hanh. Something stirred in her about her own tradition of Judaism and the spirituality and mysticism of her faith. She decided to give Judaism a chance and went to Rosh Hashanah services. The gates were opened to her faith and she was awakened.

As Rachel followed the "still small voice" speaking to her soul, she found herself on the pathway to rabbinical call and service. As she entered the rabbinate, all of her skills for organizing continued to guide her in leadership. She drew everyone into conversations and prayer about "opening the gates" for those who were locked out and kept apart. She has spent her ministry organizing people to do justice in every congregational setting. She is gifted in drawing people together to do justice. In her words, "Following the *hesed* [kindness or love] of God, we are active creating the world we want to see."

Bishop Yvette A. Flunder, the senior pastor of the City of Refuge United Church of Christ, in Oakland, California, is on assignment from God. She has been opening doors and gates closed to herself and others since she was a child. She remembers her mother lovingly saying to her as a child, "you are different." She loved stray animals. When a bird fell from a nest, she took it home, figured out how to feed it, and when it grew, let it go. She found and raised tadpoles into frogs. While all of this may seem beautifully metaphorical to you, Yvette believes she came to earth with "an assignment of empathy." I believe she is right.

Since her earliest days of life, Yvette A. Flunder has been sitting on the curb, "outside the gates" welcoming "all creatures great and small." Since 1991, City of Refuge UCC has been Bishop Flunder's location for this extravagant welcome.

The City of Refuge UCC website proclaims:

> We are intentionally radically inclusive, welcoming all persons, regardless of race, color, ancestry, age, ability, gender, sexual or affectional orientation. We celebrate the Creator's Diversity! We worship Christ and welcome people from all faith paths that harmonize with the ministry of Jesus Christ.

But the heart of empathy and compassion that the Holy Spirit has granted her is the key to the gate of refuge. Yvette has been gathering people, working together for the common good and helping heal and mend those most marginalized in our society. As she helped the little birds when she was a girl, Bishop Flunder believes God has placed her here to heal people and help them discover their assignment.

The ministry, mission, and vision of Rabbi Timoner and Bishop Flunder can be followed on their synagogue and church websites. It can be understood more deeply in their writings and preaching. I believe it comes from well-grounded biblical and experiential heart. It comes from empathy.

Dr. Brené Brown writes this of empathy: "Empathy has no script. There is no right way or wrong way to do it. It's simply listening, holding space, withholding judgment, emotionally connecting, and communicating that incredibly healing message of 'You're not alone.'"

While the terminology of "holding space" may be contemporary, the concept is as ancient as our sacred Scriptures. Through the holy encounter with the woman from Samaria, Jesus created a safe space that was free of judgment and, instead, cultivated an experience of connection, vulnerability, acceptance, trust, and unconditional love (John 4). The God of Abraham "held space" for God's people seeking home when God provided daily manna from heaven for forty years in the mountainous desert of Sinai.

Truthfully, God is "on assignment" throughout Holy Scripture, living, breathing, moving, calling, accepting, trusting, connecting, providing, loving, caring, showing the pathway to freedom and justice.

The empathetic nature of God is embodied in all of the geniuses of justice in this project. They have encountered the pain of people and all inhabitants of the planet. They have held hands, shed tears, embraced fully, and made holy space for those whom they have encountered on this journey. They embrace others with love and grace. They are poets and preachers. They are prophets and change agents. But they all "held space" for others along the way.

Two more special agents of grace on assignment from God to change this world and open the gates to everyone are Sr. Simone Campbell, SSS, and Rev. Sarah Marsh. Sr. Simone Campbell is a nun in the Sisters of Social Service (SSS) and recently retired as the executive director of NETWORK. In July 2022, Sr. Simone received the Presidential Medal of Freedom from the White House. Rev. Sarah Marsh is a pastor in the United Methodist Church and recently started in her new role as the Great Plains' Mercy and Justice coordinator for the Great Plains Conference, UMC.

Sr. Simone Campbell was born Mary Campbell in Santa Monica, California in 1945. She was inspired to live out her faith as "the fruit of first communion." In her book, *A Nun on the Bus* (2014), she wrote of her first eucharistic encounter: "There was this explosion for me. At the time I didn't fully understand it. I just knew I felt different. It was if I was just being freed of something. That feeling, that sense, that definition of Eucharist, has never really left me, and I consider that one of the great graces of my life."

The mystical presence of Christ that started for her in second grade at first Communion didn't end there. By third grade, Mary was organizing children and in fifth grade she established the Copy Cat Club to help the fifth-grade girls overcome the bossy sixth-grade girls who were bullying their younger schoolmates. They petitioned the school principal and the administration for their own part of the playground and they won. She has been organizing ever since.

During our conversation, Sr. Simone told of the test to her faith when she was a senior in high school. Her sister, Katy, then a sophomore, was diagnosed with Hodgkin's lymphoma. The disease can be treated now, but in the 1960s it was terminal, and Katy was given three to five years to live. Mary (Simone) was devastated and changed forever by her sister's illness unto death.

Katy came home from the hospital just in time for the family to be transfixed by the news coverage of the civil rights marches in Birmingham, Alabama, where protesting children were attacked by police dogs and sprayed by high-pressure fire hoses. Inspired by the young protesters, both teenagers dedicated their lives to civil rights, even as Katy's strength faded.

Sr. Simone wrote in *A Nun on the Bus*, "It just seeped into my bones, this sense that I needed to live intensely enough for both of us, to channel her passion as well as mine. As she grew weaker, my commitment only grew stronger. This wasn't a conscious process for me, at the time or since. But it certainly fed what has become my rather enthusiastic approach to life, and to living." Katy Campbell died four years later. Simone stays connected in spirit to her younger sister to this day.

On September 8, 1964, a year after graduating from high school, Campbell entered the Sisters of Social Service. Novices were allowed to suggest their own religious names, and Campbell chose "Simone," a feminizing of Simon Peter, her patron saint. "Like Peter, I can be impetuous," Campbell wrote in her latest book, *Hunger for Hope*. "I have been known to leap into situations and then have second thoughts. For me, the story of Jesus walking on the water demonstrates that in the face of 'headwinds' faith can make all the difference."

Sr. Simone is guided every day by a heart of prayer and the movement of the Holy Spirit in her life. Her daily prayer is that we all receive what we need. She listens to the poor and the forsaken in this world like few others. She lives in the present moment and gives all she has to God in service and in love.

As I have known Sr. Simone across the years, she has always touched my heart by the way in which she lives fully for others. If you will, she lives for two as she carries the spirit of Katy in all she says and does. Sr. Simone lives deeply in the spirit of God. She stands at the gates and opens them wide and will do so—for two—until God calls her home to the gates of glory.

Rev. Sarah Marsh is a native of Halstead in south central Kansas. A United Methodist pastor, Rev. Marsh said her heart for mercy and justice began developing in high school after a mission trip to a Mexican orphanage. "The kids I got to know and the situation of their lives really exposed me to a different world," she said. "I've been in contact with those kids, who are now adults and having babies of their own over the last couple of decades, and just feel passionately concerned about the needs of the world and those who struggle."

As we talked, Sarah told the story of eight-year-old Rolando. She met him on her first mission trip in the slums of Monterrey, Mexico when she was fifteen years old. In the absolute pandemonium of her mission group's arrival in the slums, Rolando looked her in the eyes and said, "I am hungry." Knowing there were many hungry children close at hand, and knowing that to feed one meant to feed them all and she wasn't in charge, Sarah looked in Rolando's eyes and said, "I can't give you food." She says, "In that moment, I felt the anguish of God over the pain of the world. I gave myself to God and said, 'I am yours.' In Matthew 25, I meet Christ as I meet the people who are in need. I cannot walk away from the needs of God's people after I have met Christ in them."

Sarah has returned to Mexico across her lifetime. She returned as a teen and then as a teacher. She served in the "City of Children." Then, as part of a Human Rights delegation, Sarah visited the Mayan village of Acteal, in Chiapas, where on December 22, 1997, forty-five people were massacred by a right-wing paramilitary group while attending a prayer meeting of indigenous townspeople in a small Catholic church. Included in the massacre were children and pregnant women who were members of the pacifist group Las Abejas ("The Bees"). In September, 2020, the Mexican government finally admitted responsibility for the massacre. During her visit, Sarah met the survivors of the massacre who live with the deep scars of machete cuts on their faces. She felt God saying, "Come and see. This is what my work looks like in the belly of the beast." Sarah continued, "I saw Christ again. He was slaughtered with them. He died with them there in the chapel."

Sarah decided to return to the United States to dedicate her life to work "on the ground" where she was in Kansas. She has done that as a pastor and a community organizer. There she has given her life in trying to be effective with JUMP in Topeka, Kansas, and now by organizing and leading congregations in the Great Plains Conference.

The genius of Sarah Marsh is vast and deep. She connects her passion to address racism, the abusive power of men over women, and the stigmatization of sexuality with the injustices she encounters on the streets of Topeka and Wichita, Acteal and Monterrey. Sarah thinks globally and acts locally. She doesn't want to look into the eyes of Rolando or any other girl or boy and say again, "I can't give you food" in a nation and world where there is enough food to feed everyone. Paraphrasing Walter Brueggemann, Sarah says, "We have to figure what belongs to whom and return it to those from whom it has been taken." She concludes, "I will not rest until everyone has enough."

Rabbi Rachel, Bishop Yvette, Sr. Simone, and Rev. Sarah are four women geniuses of justice. They are four women on assignments from God. They have opened the gates of righteousness. They have taken their places with those who have been shut out, locked out, kept out, hurt, wounded, abandoned, and starved in a world where this should never happen. None of them will rest until everyone has enough.

I ask this as you read: "Did you open the gates?" If yes, thank you. If not, why not? Will you join me and look out your window tonight? Make a decision which side of the gates you will be on. You will find your sisters are already on the other side of the gates binding the broken. Join them there. They are all on assignments from God. They are witnessing for more than themselves. They are welcoming and loving. They are holding space for those who have been cut off and cut out of economies that turn their backs on invisible multitudes of women, children, and men who struggle in poverty. They are embracing each day in the collaborative and cooperative work for justice. They are opening the gates of God to all who have been locked out for too long.

## Reflection to Action Questions:

1. Like Rabbi Rachel Timoner, how have you "opened the gates" for someone? How did it change your life? If you have not opened to gates, why not? How can you do it now?

2. Like Bishop Yvette Flunder, what is the "assignment" God has for your life? How will you live into it?

3. Like Sr. Simone Campbell, how do you "live your life fully for others"? Is there a way you could imagine, like Sr. Simone, that you are here to live for yourself and someone else? Who might that be?

4. Like Rev. Sarah Marsh, how can you "figure what belongs to whom and return it to those from whom it has been taken"? Will you not rest until everyone has enough?

# Chapter 9: **Raising the Dead**

*Will you come and follow me, if I but call your name?*
*Will you go where you don't know, and never be the same?*
*Will you let my love be shown, will you let my name be known,*
*Will you let my life be grown, in you and you in me?*

*Will you leave yourself behind, if I but call your name?*
*Will you care for cruel and kind, and never be the same?*
*Will you risk the hostile stare, should your life attract or scare?*
*Will you let me answer prayer, in you and you in me?*

—JOHN BELL, "THE SUMMONS"

THE CALL TO FOLLOW God into difficult and challenging places has defined many of the geniuses of justice—none more than Sr. Helen Prejean. Sr. Helen did not start out to change the world. A good young Catholic woman of the 1950s, she entered religious life with a sincere vision of saying "yes" to God in prayer. As a young sister in the Congregation of St. Joseph of Medaille, Helen dedicated her life to Jesus Christ, to teaching and a devoted life of prayer and spirituality.

From 1962 to 1982, Sr. Helen was a religious educator. She focused on spiritual formation, hours of worship and prayer, time for meditation and reflection, reading and the study of theology. In her words, "I was working to help people be good and follow Jesus. I was teaching and leading retreats. I was helping people get closer to God." For the first forty-three years of her life, she was a faithful Catholic and servant of God. There was nothing flashy about her. Nothing in any of this drew attention to her. She was simply doing her job and serving her Savior.

Then in 1982, "Sneaky Jesus" showed up. He came in the form of an acquaintance who asked her to correspond with convicted murderer Elmo Patrick Sonnier. Pat Sonnier was on death row in the Louisiana State Penitentiary, known as Angola. He had been sentenced to death by electrocution. He wrote to her, "I'm Catholic. You're a nun. You could be my spiritual advisor." After several visits, she agreed to serve as his spiritual advisor in the months leading up to his execution.

She continues, "I had been catapulted into the death chamber. Two and one-half years after writing me my first letter, Pat was killed. I thought, 'Humans can change.' I watched this man 'change in his heart' and now I watched this changed man die before my eyes. I vomited in the killing chamber."

The experience gave Sr. Helen Prejean greater insight into the process involved in executions, for the convict, families, and others in the prison, and she began speaking out against capital punishment. At the same time, she also founded *Survive*, an organization devoted to counseling the families of victims of violence.

As Sr. Helen told me, "I was in my forties before I woke up to injustice. I had to move out of the suburbs and into the 'field hospital' where the wounded are. I had to move in with a community of people who focused on justice. I discovered that hope comes to us when we are participating with it."

In 1993, she wrote *Dead Man Walking*. In the book, she drew from her experiences with Sonnier and another convict, Robert Lee Willie. In the 1995 film by the same name, Matthew Poncelet (the dead man walking) is based on Sonnier and Willie. Like Pat, Robert had been sentenced to death after being convicted of kidnapping and murder in two attacks in May 1980. Willie was an avowed Aryan, a devotee of Hitler, a racist and a misogynist. Sr. Helen dealt with all of this as she cared for him unto death.

Sr. Helen also explored the effects that conducting the death penalty has on attorneys, prison guards, other prison officials, and the families of both convicted murderers and their victims. All of these experiences and relationships have convinced her that the death penalty must end. Executions must stop.

For the past forty years, Sr. Prejean has worked with other men sentenced to death. She has also become a national spokeswoman in opposition to the death penalty. She has written three books on her life journey.

In *River of Fire* (2019), Sr. Helen tells of her first forty-three years of life and faith before her engagement with men on death row.

The true power of her story is that like all of our stories, her life is filled with gradual changes, unexpected encounters, and uncomfortable new beginnings. With Sr. Helen, we see that there is no one, singular point of decision in a life of faith. It is a constant movement of conversion, growth, and change—always guided by the Holy Spirit, the Spirit of fire! For her, the key is opening our hearts to the movement of the Spirit at work in us each day.

Sr. Helen exudes love and joy. She cares about the prisoners on death row. She cares about their victims. She cares about the families of the victims and the families of the inmates. She cares about the attorneys involved in all these cases. She cares about the guards, the other employees in the prison system, and the other inmates held captive. She prays with and for all of them.

Sr. Helen calls for restorative justice. She says, "When harm is done to one member of the community, the whole community is wounded. We need to gather and restore the whole community. We do not address the root of violence and what must be done to make for healthy and healing relationships. Instead, we run a system we call 'the Justice System,' which is really just the State vs. the Criminal—and that is not justice."

She continues, "When we see the divine likeness and power in one another, then we open the unlimited capacity to know the truth and love that is always resting within us. We awaken within. The Spirit is moving deepest when we are awakened. God resides there. It is in that moment, in that time, that you come to know the true presence of God. The energy of God flows through us. Life and vibrancy flow through us."

Sr. Helen continues to pay close attention to Sneaky Jesus. Just as the risen Christ presented himself to Peter at the seaside so long ago in the Gospel of John, chapter 21, he surprises us today. He shows up when we are least expecting his visit. He calls us to love and follow. The places he calls us to are often places to which we would rather not go. It is in moments of call that we discover who we really are.

As John Bell writes in his hymn "The Summons," "Will you come and follow me, if I but call your name? Will you go where you don't know, and never be the same?" Sr. Helen is always open to God's call in her life. She says, "God moved me to another place and changed me forever. I am forever thankful to God for this."

This spiritual call to follow God into the most difficult places is in the bones and spirit of many of the geniuses of justice.

Pastor Shane Claiborne is half the age of Sr. Helen. He awakened half a lifetime ago as well. Shane has worked tirelessly for justice since his teenage years. He has focused on gun violence and the death penalty, among other projects for peace and justice. "Justice is what love looks like in public," Shane says, quoting Cornel West. This comes into clear focus with the death penalty. "We kill people to show that killing people is wrong. That's crazy. We don't rape people to show that raping people is wrong," he says. He goes on to say that Jesus suffered the death penalty in his time at the hands of the Roman Empire. As his followers, we all need to oppose the crucifixion of people in our time. "Jesus and justice operate the way the blades of scissors work—they always operate together to cut through injustice."

Shane believes capital punishment needs to go for good in the United States—a country that's in company with China, Iran, Saudi Arabia, Iraq, and Egypt for countries with the highest execution rates. We execute justice primarily against Black people and poor people. We are literally killing the poorest of the poor. While only 13 percent of Americans are Black, close to 50 percent of men and women on death row are Black. But that has been true since the beginning of executions. Bryan Stevenson takes Claiborne's point one step further.

He writes in *Just Mercy*:

> The reality is that capital punishment in America is a lottery. It is a punishment that is shaped by the constraints of poverty, race, geography and local politics.

These constraints of poverty, race, geography, and local politics weave their way through our history in an evil tapestry of hate. Throughout our history Black people have been executed by the state at an alarming rate. This does not even include more than 6,400 lynchings that took place between 1865 and 1950. Since 1950, the murder of Black men and women continued unabated. Vigilantes and Klansmen were the (mostly uncharged) killers of forty-one people slain during the civil rights movement alone.

One of the most remarkable "call stories" for a genius of justice is the story of Bryan Stevenson. Mr. Stevenson was not available for a conversation for this project, but I feel strongly a need to incorporate him in this chapter. Stevenson and his staff's remarkable efforts through the Equal Justice Initiative (EJI) have won reversals and release from prison for over 135 wrongly condemned prisoners on death row and won relief for hundreds of others wrongly convicted or unfairly sentenced.

Growing up in the Prospect African Methodist Episcopal Church, Bryan was grounded in Christian faith. He was shaped by his faith in Jesus. His maternal grandfather was stabbed to death in a robbery gone wrong when Bryan was sixteen years old. This deeply affected him. The killers received life sentences, an outcome Stevenson thought fair. Stevenson said of the murder: "Because my grandfather was older, his murder seemed particularly cruel. But I came from a world where we valued redemption over revenge."

Going to Harvard Law School following college at Eastern University (where Shane Claiborne attended as well), Bryan dedicated his life to caring for those unjustly incarcerated. His dedication to men and women on death row has been remarkable.

In *Just Mercy: A Story of Justice and Redemption,* Stevenson writes:

> Proximity has taught me some basic and humbling truths, including this vital lesson: Each of us is more than the worst thing we've ever done. My work with the poor and the incarcerated has persuaded me that the opposite of poverty is not wealth; the opposite of poverty is justice. Finally, I've come to believe that the true measure of our commitment to justice, the character of our society, our commitment to the rule of law, fairness, and equality cannot be measured by how we treat the rich, the powerful, the privileged, and the respected among us. The true measure of our character is how we treat the poor, the disfavored, the accused, the incarcerated, and the condemned.

Stevenson goes on to say, that "simply punishing the broken—walking away from them or hiding them from sight—only ensures that they remain broken and we do, too. There is no wholeness outside of our reciprocal humanity."

For those of us who are Christian, we belong to a community of faith now more than two thousand years old grounded in justice and mercy, forgiveness and grace. We follow a Savior who raised the dead and was raised from the dead. We say we believe in raising the dead. Having witnessed our innocent Jesus lynched on a cross on trumped-up charges, we should all be fighting every day for the abolition of the death penalty. We need to fight for the "dead men and women walking" today.

We know some things about death penalty cases. We know that for cases whose outcomes are known, an astonishing 82 percent of retried death row inmates turned out not to deserve the death penalty; 7 percent were not guilty. We know this process takes nine years on average. Put simply, most death verdicts are too flawed to carry out, and most flawed ones are scrapped for good.

Since we know that at least 7 percent of those cases retried were found not guilty of the crime for which they were sent to death row and we know 82 percent deserved not to receive the death penalty, why do we keep it going? If we knew that seven out of every one hundred planes going up in the air each day couldn't fly, we would not lift those planes into flight. If we knew that seven out of every one hundred cars coming off the assembly line would have failed brakes and crash within the first hundred miles of driving, those cars would never leave the plant where they were made. Why then, do we continue to push the death penalty in a system of injustice that is literally designed with fatal flaws?

It is time to stop killing people to show that killing people is wrong. We need to follow the geniuses of justice and not the slogans of capital punishers. We are called to "raise the dead" and save the living. In the spirit of Helen, Shane, and Bryan, let us raise the dead.

## Reflection to Action Questions:

1. Sr. Helen's story is one of awakening. She literally changed midlife. As she says, "Sneaky Jesus" shook her foundations and turned her around. Reflect on her awakening. Have you been changed by a letter, a call, a conversation? How has this happened in your life? If not, is it possible you never put yourself in a place where you could possibly encounter God's transforming presence? If not, why not?

2. Shane Claiborne is a provocative radical Christian who provides prayerful insights and analysis to make change in this world. How could you engage his writings and challenges for change?

3. Bryan Stevenson has literally saved one life after another. Watch (it has been made into a film) or read *Just Mercy* and you will witness a man who changes and then dedicates his life to "raise the dead." What do you think about this? How can you join in local, statewide, or national efforts to "raise the dead" and end the death penalty?

# Section 4—**What Matters in the Work of Justice**

# Chapter 10: **Racism and Pain Matter— Moving against Time**

*Because even if I should speak, no one would believe me. And they would not believe me precisely because they would know that what I said was true.*

—James Baldwin

*If the majority knew the root of this evil,
then the road to its cure would not be long.*

—Albert Einstein

*What have you done? Your brother's blood cries out to me from the ground!*

—Genesis 4:10

Otis Moss Jr., the son of Magnolia and Otis Moss Sr., and the fourth of their five children, was raised in LaGrange in Troup County, Georgia. Born in February 1935, Otis Jr. was only two years old when Mitchell Moss, known as Grandpa Mitchell, died.

Grandpa Mitchell was born into slavery in Merriweather County, Georgia in 1861. Freed from slavery at four years old, Mitchell rose in freedom, successfully running his agricultural business and accumulating 1,100 acres of farm land across his lifetime. When the Great Depression hit, Mitchell had his land taken from him by white businessmen and government officials. He was swindled as he mortgaged part of the land to help his family survive in the depths of the Depression. Then all his land was taken when he "defaulted" on a loan. He died with very little to show for a lifetime of hard work and entrepreneurial brilliance.

However, Grandpa Mitchell's powerful story of rising in freedom is embedded in the Moss family oral tradition. Several years ago, Otis Jr. preached at Branch Hebron Baptist Church in Odessadale, Georgia, where Grandpa Mitchell had been a deacon. And there in the cornerstone of the church building originally founded by former slaves in 1868, Otis Jr. found Mitchell Moss's name. He was a founder and builder of Branch Hebron Baptist Church. No one could take that away from him.

Growing up in rural Georgia, it was family, church, and the African American community that were *the* three pillars in the early life of Otis Moss Jr. Each was a sustaining force. And each was under constant attack. The family was constantly demoralized as fathers and mothers struggled to provide housing, food, and opportunities for their children. The church was a powerful witness for God. But whenever and wherever a Black pastor addressed economic and racial inequality, the church was burned or bombed. And Black schools at the heart of the community were, in the words of Otis Moss Jr., "inadequately supplied, criminally neglected, structurally dilapidated and filled with too many children in too small a space. In spite of that, each day my school was filled with affirmation and love."

With family, church, and community under persistent, vitriolic racist attacks, each institution found a way to overcome what was happening. Otis says, "Each was a carrier of the liberation motif. They embodied faith, hope, and love so that in the worst circumstances a song, a sermon, a lesson, a prayer, a prophetic voice kept coming on." Dr. Moss continues, "Often spoken in a language that only our Black community understood, 'ain't gonna let nobody turn us around,' we sung from deep in our souls. We were marching up to Calvary. We were marching up to freedom land. Nothing could stop us."

The Rev. Dr. Otis Moss Jr. is an iconic leader for our times and for all time. But he is not the only voice who spoke to the sting and pain of racism.

Bishop Lafayette Scales had moved to a new neighborhood and a new school not long after his father died. From the predominantly Black neighborhood in East Columbus to a white neighborhood on the north side of the city, the change was huge for the eight-year-old child. He missed his old friends and the familiarity of his former community. When one of his new classmates asked for his phone number, young Lafayette was happy to share it. That night, when the phone rang it was for him. He was excited to hear from his new classmate. When he took the phone and put the receive to his ear, the voice on the other end spewed hateful, racist vitriol at him. He was shattered. His mother said, "Don't give your phone number to kids at school again." He faced a prejudicial awakening at an early age.

Dr. John Perkins was raised by his grandparents, who were share-croppers in New Hebron, Mississippi. In the 1930s, John Perkins knew firsthand the wrath of racism. His brother Clyde was murdered by a white police officer when John was seventeen. John fled to California to escape a similar fate. In 1970, he was arrested and then tortured by white police officers. His crime? He had been in a peaceful protest march boycotting white businesses in Mendenhall, Mississippi. He emerged from this to form a ministry of holistic healing seeking ways to heal the racial divides. When we talked, John Perkins asked, "Who was it that 'color coded' skin? It certainly was not God. So that leaves Man. What Man has done is not acceptable in the eyes of God. There is absolutely no question—racism is a sin. And the problems that humanity has created to keep us apart will always stand under the judgment of God."

Rev. Charles Heyward grew up on St. John's Island, South Carolina. As a sophomore, he transferred to a high school where he was the only Black male. Charles had been a gifted scholar and athlete at his all-Black school. In the new high school, he experienced three years of hell even though he was better at sports and academics than most of the students. He held the long jump record for twenty-eight years. It didn't matter. He endured racial hate—as he was spat on in the face, hit in the face, kicked everywhere on his body, physically abused, and called every imaginable crafty use and abuse of the "n-word" than he ever thought possible. He learned the hard way, "There are certain things you cannot react to that will expose your hurt. It will bring you more pain."

James "Papa" Kee, Rev. Dr. Jefferey P. Kee's father, escaped Birming-ham, Alabama in the Great Migration, having had his life threatened a number of times for the "crime" of being Black in Birmingham. As a Black man in Birmingham, James Kee would regularly face racial abuse. The police would raid school dances and threaten the young men with their lives. One time leaving Birmingham at the train station he was accused of calling a white police officer a name. When he denied it, his life was threatened at gunpoint by the officer who kept screaming at him, "Are you a ni***r?" When he would not say "yes," the officer kept pushing the gun against his head. Finally, his sister screamed at the officer, "He is a ni***r! Let that poor ni***r live!"

James survived this near-death encounter. He settled in Columbus, Ohio, but he could not escape the tentacles of racism and tragedy. His oldest son was gunned down and killed by "friends" on the streets of Columbus. His youngest son and daughters have all spent a lifetime dealing with their brother's violent death and the daily challenges of being Black in Columbus. Jefferey has dedicated his life to fighting for justice in Columbus.

The Rev. Dr. Joseph Owens grew up in Lebanon, Kentucky. It is a town divided by railroad tracks. He grew up on "the other side of the tracks." There was a white side of town and a Black side of town. When he was forced, at nine years old, to go to the white school when his school closed, Joe was very angry. He did not want to be anywhere near white people. One year later, after a hellacious year in school, Joe befriended some white boys. When they all decided to go to the movie theater, he was, as always, forced to sit in the balcony. His white friends refused to leave his side. They soon found out their seats were accompanied by rats jumping across your feet during the movies. They were horrified. But they did not abandon Joe. That bonding experience turned around his view of white people and started friendships that endure to this day.

In these stories you hear of theft of 1,100 acres of land accrued over a lifetime, church burnings and bombings, murder and torture, beatings and abuse, verbal abuse of a child, physical and emotional harassment, threats of murder, and racial divides all because of "color lines." Slavery, racism, and racial violence have criminally altered lives and disrupted and destroyed families for over four hundred years.

Besides these six Black men who shared these painful and difficult stories of racism, the other twelve Black women and men in this project also tied their life experiences with racism and racial injustice all the way back to childhood. One thing was clear in the depth and breadth of the conversations. When I asked, "How did you become who you are today?" all eighteen African American geniuses went back to childhood and personal familial memories to share painful racist and discriminatory experiences that eventually shaped who they became. Besides Moss, Scales, Perkins, Heyward, Kee, and Owens, Marian Wright Edelman, Yvette Flunder, Terry Green, Obrey Hendricks Jr., Ralph Hodge, Adrienne Hood, Melissa McFadden, Otis Moss III, Bobby Rush, Donald Washington, Starsky Wilson, and

Jeremiah Wright all shared stories, too. Many of these stories are chronicled in other chapters.

Most of the other thirty-five geniuses of justice identified painful life experiences as the fire that forged and shaped them into who they are today. Fighting through the inclination to give up and give in to bitterness when faced with racist hate and/or painful memories, the fifty-three forged hope and a vision for a better world from experiences of racial discrimination and personal pain.

While a number of the Jewish geniuses shared early memories of anti-semitism, almost all of the non-African American geniuses talked of "awakening" experiences to racial injustice as they became teens and young adults. Some spoke of youth mission trips to poor urban neighborhoods across America, while others spoke of a range of Third World countries. Many remembered books, stories, friendships, or classes in college that changed their worldview and set them on a course of justice action. While injustice was clearly experiential and real life for *all* of the Black geniuses and was rooted in generations of close and painful family stories, for the predominance of white geniuses, exposure to racial injustice was learned.

I have thought of this often while writing this chapter. Is it any wonder why so many white people are so clueless to the visceral pain of racism when it is literally so far from their life experience? James Baldwin's words echo through my mind: "Because even if I should speak, no one would believe me. And they would not believe me precisely because they would know that what I said was true."

Moreover, God's question to Cain in Genesis 4:10 plays on repeat. "What have you done? Your brother's blood cries out to me from the ground!"

If you don't believe that your brother's blood cries out from the ground, talk with Adrienne Hood. Each day, she lives without her son Henry Green V, who was murdered by Columbus police on the streets in Linden, his neighborhood, on June 6, 2016. Henry was twenty-three years old at the time of his murder. In the year following the lynching of George Floyd on the streets of Minneapolis, Minnesota, 229 Black and brown Americans were killed by police in our nation. It was as if the heinous murder of one Black man by police unleashed open season for police everywhere in the racist war against people of color anywhere. God is still weeping: "What have you done?"

I shared my discovery of experiential versus learned encounters with racial injustice with Black friends and colleagues. They all agreed this matches their experience, too. They have found that white people rarely have experienced life-shaping and soul-crushing pain in relation to injustice while almost all of their Black friends and family have encountered hardship in relation to racial injustice.

When I asked them what needs to be heard and shared, they added their insights. Fred said, "Tim, tell the truth about this." Jefferey added, "For over four hundred years, African Americans have suffered from the effects of constant and continual abuse and the residual effect of PTSD—post-traumatic stress syndrome—because our life story in America is packed with trauma and stress. Until we treat the cancer of racism, we will always battle the side effects and aftereffects of its violence." One friend said, "tell people that is not what you *say* but what you *do* that matters. How do you treat people in the workplace, in your neighborhood, at school, and in daily interactions? That is what matters." Ray said, "What also matters is that we see the larger issues of racism—the systemic injustices that prevail to this day. It is not enough to treat people well (although that is greatly appreciated). It is about changing systems that block advancement, opportunity, dignity, and equity." Kevin said, "Always remember that race itself is a social construct. It is not a real thing. So, everything that follows is built on bad science and destructive systemic injustice. Also, we all need to remember and celebrate the great achievements of Black Americans who have led our nation in every single area of our life together. There is literally no area where Black Americans have not made advances and a significant difference in our nation's story." Thank you, friends. And amen.

My African American friends and all the geniuses of justice are focused on overcoming the painful racial injustices all around us. Now, we have to join Albert Einstein and bring the majority of Americans into the battle against racial injustice.

There are more than four hundred years of genuine and justifiable anger in the soul of Black America. In August 2019, I shared a six-part sermon series with three African American colleagues entitled "Four Hundred Years of Africans in America." The scourge of American slavery and the mistreatment of Black people in our land started in August 1619 as the White Lion, the first slave ship known in the colonies, arrived at Point Comfort, what is now Hampton, Virginia.

In what I call the true founding document of this nation, the manifest of the White Lion, it records that "20 and odd" Africans had been captured from the slave ship *San Juan Bautista* in a fierce battle in the Bay of Campeche in the Gulf of Mexico and now were for sale in our land. We know two names—Antonio and Isabella. We know them only because they appear later in the records of their slave owner. The other names are unknown. There was no true accounting for the evil beginnings of slavery in America. This manifest needs to be placed in the National Archives next to the Declaration of Independence, the Constitution, and the Bill of Rights. It is a founding document of our nation.

For more than four hundred years, we have reaped what we have sown and these seeds of racism, bigotry, and hate continue to be sown and reaped today. The fifty-three geniuses of justice in this project have all dedicated their lives to harvesting justice and not hate. The men and women I spoke with are leaders in confronting the machinery of systematic violence and injustice that African Americans endure every day. They do it in many ways and in many places. They work on policies that call for the flourishing of all children—especially those who have been left behind by inequities in American life. They fight for health care protections for minority women, men, and families. They address mental health concerns and prenatal health care—among other health crises in poor and minority communities. They fight for equal education and against the burning and banning of books and historic truth and the bizarre right-wing attack on critical race theory. They fight against redlining and fight for fair housing and justice for low-income people who need safe, secure, and affordable housing. They fight police brutality and the criminal justice system that is unjustly designed to incarcerate and kill Black and brown people. They work on public transportation issues, immigration rights, capital punishment, and more.

All fifty-three geniuses of justice have connected the dots of racial prejudice and pain to design and bring to fruition a better world of love and justice.

In his book *How to Be an Antiracist*, Ibram X. Kendi identifies the struggle we are all in as "the struggle to be fully human and to see that others are fully human." He continues that we can no longer pretend to be "not racist." "Not racist" is not a thing. He says you either choose to be racist or antiracist. You have to make a choice. To be antiracist takes education and a lifetime commitment to change policies and practices of racist structures and mores. I have chosen to live each day of my life as an antiracist. Some days I do better than others. But it is a lifetime commitment. What will your choice be? Will you be a racist or an antiracist?

Into the mix of racism and pain comes Isabel Wilkerson and her groundbreaking 2020 book, *Caste: The Origins of Our Discontents*. In *Caste*, Wilkerson tells the story of Rev. Dr. Martin Luther King Jr.'s pilgrimage to India in the winter of 1959. Dr. King went on a pilgrimage to see the land of Mahatma Gandhi, the father of nonviolent protests. Dr. King had recently finished leading the yearlong Montgomery bus boycott in Alabama and now he wanted to meet the people whose battle against the oppressive rule of Great Britain had inspired his own fight for justice in America. During his monthlong stay, at the invitation of prime minster Jawaharlal Nehru, he sought out the so-called untouchables, the lowest caste in the ancient Indian caste system.

Isabel Wilkerson takes us to the southern tip of India, to the city of Trivandrum in the state of Kerala. There, Martin and Coretta Scott King visited high school students whose families had been Untouchables. The principal introduced Dr. King this way: "Young people, I would like to present to you a fellow untouchable from the United States of America."

In Wilkerson's words, "King was floored. He had not expected the term to be applied to him. He was, in fact, put off by it at first. He had flown in from another continent, had dined with the prime minister . . . and 'For a moment,' he wrote, 'I was a bit shocked and peeved that I would be referred to as an untouchable.'" Then he began to think of the reality of the twenty million people consigned to the lowest rank of American society for centuries. In his words, "We were still smothering in an airtight cage of poverty, quarantined in isolated ghettos, exiled in our own country." Finally, he said to himself, "Yes, I am an untouchable, and every Negro in the United States of America is an untouchable."

More than sixty years ago, in a high school in Trivandrum, India, Dr. King came to realize the truth of the America system of caste—Black people in America are treated almost exactly like the untouchables of India. We also have a caste system in America. He would speak to it in the final years of his life, but it was not a major theme of his speaking or writing. It took the brilliant research and expository writing of Isabel Wilkerson to uncover and reveal the long and twisted history of caste in America.

Caste is the unseen structure of systemic injustice in America. America is an old house built on a faulty foundation with an infrastructure of caste. Wilkerson writes, "Caste and race are neither synonymous nor mutually exclusive. They can and do coexist in the same culture and serve to reinforce each other. Race, in the United States, is the visible agent of the unseen force of caste. Caste is the bones, race the skin. Race is what we can see, the physical traits that have been given arbitrary meaning and become shorthand for who a person is. Caste is the powerful infrastructure that holds each group in its place."

The "untouchable" Dr. King, in all his brilliant, provocative, and powerful ways, was able to recognize this long before most people did. He was not the first to write or speak about the structure of our old house whose foundation stones were laid in 1619. Ashley Montagu (1942) and Gunnar Myrdal (1944) wrote books about our caste system. Bhimrao Ambedkar, an Indian untouchable who came to America to study economics in 1913, wrote about this. He reached out to meet and talk with W. E. B. DuBois. DuBois had already written about these comparisons. Together, Ambedkar and he were able to develop these concepts and comparisons. Ambedkar rejected the term *untouchables* and even the term *Harijans* given to his people by Gandhi. He chose to call his own people *Dalits,* which means "broken people." He saw the pain and brokenness of his own people and felt they needed their own word to name and claim their reality.

Caste is the bones. Race is the skin. The bones of America are broken. Our system is broken. Black Americans are broken by this old house built in sand on a four-hundred-plus–year-old foundation of injustice. We need to rebuild a nation based on a rock-solid foundation of justice for *all.*

It will take all of us naming each of the broken bones in our structure of injustice to begin to build a just body. Let us take the discovery of the untouchable Dr. King and the revelations of the incredible Isabel Wilkerson to name our caste system for what it is. Then we can build a new house on a solid foundation of justice and human equality.

On the walls of my study, there are eight beautiful pictures of African American women and men. They are: Breonna Taylor, Riah Milton, Oluwatoyin Salau, Hank Aaron, Jackie Robinson, Satchel Paige, Bill Willis Sr., and Jefferey P. Kee. Breonna, Riah, and Oluwatoyin are martyrs of violence against women of color. Hank, Jackie, and Satchel are my sports heroes from baseball—America's greatest game. Bill Willis Sr. broke the color barrier in pro football in 1946 and was a second father to me. Jefferey is my brother. The loving spirits and memories of these women and men remind me daily of the millions who battle against racism and injustice. They inspire me to stay on the path of anti-racism. They guide my steps each day in the battle against our caste system and the racial injustice and inequities that are embedded in it.

I implore everyone who reads this chapter to vow to be an antiracist beginning in this moment. Even if you have not experienced racism and caste firsthand, you live in this old house and you know they are real. Also, you have known pain. You know what it feels like to hurt and be hurt. Acknowledging pain and the hardship tens of millions of Black Americans have faced, make choices that bring new life and hope to others who have experienced the pain of racism and caste in America. Remember the names of Antonio and Isabella. When they arrived in August 1619, along with "20 and odd" other Africans, they became our ancestors in this American life. We need to honor our ancestors forevermore.

Remember these words from Fannie Lou Hamer: "There are two things we should never forget. We should never forget where we came from and the bridges that carried us over." This truth is for all of us, not just some of us.

## Reflection to Action Questions:

1. These words settle into our soul—"Caste is the bones. Race is the skin." How do you reflect on our "old America house" built on a foundation of injustice?

2. What about these stories told by those who have felt the pain of racism and the pain of injustice? What touches you about their stories?

3. As a white man, I know that I can walk away from these issues of racial injustice any day at any time. That is white privilege. It's real. I have made a vow to be an antiracist every day. No matter the color of your skin, how will you live your life as an antiracist? What will you do today? Tomorrow? The next day? And on and on, one day at a time?

# Chapter 11: **Inclusion Matters— Leaving No One Behind**

*And the king will answer them, "Truly I tell you, just as you did it to one of the least of these who are members of my family, you did it to me."*

—MATTHEW 25:40

REV. DR. J. BENNETT Guess was organizing for children's rights when he was a ten-year-old growing up in Henderson, Kentucky. He set up an organization called Kids Need Rights Too (KNRT). As a KNRT spokesperson, he would go on speaking tours addressing issues of bullying and taunting. His public service announcement "Won't You Help?" was used far and wide. Between the ages ten and fifteen, Ben committed himself to addressing issues of child abuse and child neglect. As a gay child, he knew a lot about bullying and taunting. The children he was defending and protecting were often like him. They were facing ridicule and abuse for simply being gay or lesbian.

Ben was also well versed in public policy and law. Dinner table conversations always explored the news, ideas for social change, abortion, the death penalty, and more. By ten years old he also had memorized all the federal cabinet positions and who served on president Jimmy Carter's cabinet. As a young Christian growing up in the South, President Carter's deep Christian values meant a lot to Ben. He was, in Ben's words, "a true Christian." Not only that, Jimmy Carter had campaigned in Henderson, Kentucky and Ben knew people who could call Jimmy Carter directly. He felt like he had one degree of separation from the president of the United States. He felt like his church was a "country club church"—never pushing the edges on justice issues. The church seemed like no option for doing justice, so he turned to law with an eye to politically elected office. He was prelaw at the University of Kentucky and deeply involved with the College

Democrats. He even worked for a law firm beginning in his freshman year and continuing on through college.

Ben's vocational path in law seemed all set until he had a "born again experience." His mind and spirit were transformed as he read an introduction to liberation theology by the Brazilian theologian Leonardo Boff. Ben says, "It was the first time I ever understood that the gospel of Jesus Christ is for liberation. I then saw my Christian faith in a radically different way." Shortly after, as a junior in college, Ben came out to people as gay. He was a gay Christian activist. As such, he headed to seminary at Vanderbilt Divinity School. He was a gay Methodist serving student pastorates in Western Kentucky. He had a four-point charge (meaning he served four little congregations at one time). He spent three years in seminary serving these four churches in which he preached five times each week. Because the Methodist *Book of Discipline* does not allow for the ordination of gay people, Ben could not be "out" in the United Methodist Church. After seminary, he served one and one-half years in the denomination, where he was closeted at church but not in the rest of his life. He could no longer abide in this two-tier world.

He came into the United Church of Christ through an Ecclesiastical Council of one hundred people who accepted him into the denomination by only seven votes. However, the twelve members of Zion United Church of Christ in his hometown of Henderson, Kentucky received him with open arms. For the next eight years, Ben would lead Zion to become the first open and affirming congregation in Kentucky. It also became a just peace church. During their eight years together, the congregation grew from twelve to three hundred members. Worship attendance grew from a handful to four weekly services, filling the little church. And their mission grew, too. Guided by Matthew 25 and Jesus' call to care for the poor and serve our neighbors in need, Zion's mission and purpose grew exponentially—including a strong HIV/AIDS ministry.

Since leaving Zion UCC in 2000, Ben has risen through the years to become one of the top leaders in the United Church of Christ and now serves as the executive director of the ACLU in Ohio. In the midst of a life committed to justice, Ben has remained faithful to his call to follow the liberating Jesus. For Ben, justice is seeking right relationships with all humankind and all creation.

Inspired by theologian Carter Heyward, he follows a theology of mutuality. He says, "We are siblings in Christ who are called to be in right relations with the world we are trying to create." He is driven by a belief that we are called to be kind. He says, "Kindness really matters to me. While kindness is not the completion of the gospel, the gospel will never be complete without it." Moreover, Ben says, "When we become unkind and apathetic, we lose track of God's call to racial justice and inclusion. We need to move out of comfort zones in justice and take on the needs of others who don't look like us. This crossover of people and causes will be for our healing and where we will build hope."

J. Bennett Guess is an inspirational inclusive leader. He has spent his life building bridges between the gay and straight community, the white and Black community, and the Christian and non-Christian community. He has been my teacher in the ways of inclusion and kindness.

Rev. Dr. Loey Powell has been a champion of inclusion as an ordained minister of the United Church of Christ. She has been a trailblazer in the denomination and the Christian world. Loey grew up in Oak Park, Illinois in the 1960s as a preacher's kid. Her father was a pastor who was very engaged in civil rights and her mother was "a feisty rulebreaker." Organizing for open housing with rabbis and other ministers in Oak Park, her father faced threats from angry white neighbors and they even had their phones tapped. Loey was surrounded by activists in her home and church. The student seminarians who served the congregation took the teens into the South Side of Chicago, introducing them to impoverished communities where real liberation struggles were happening and the Black Panthers were actively organizing for change. As she headed to Oberlin College, she was awakened even more to the anti-war movement, feminism, and liberation theology as a student in religion. That fall, she was knocked down by the death of her younger brother. She took time to heal from her brother Joe's death at seventeen. As she was healing, she took time away before returning to finish at Oberlin.

In the years that followed, Loey continued to explore her spirituality and faith. In time, she found herself at Pacific School of Religion (PSR). There she fell in love. There she continued her growth as a feminist and liberation theologian. She was active in the Center for Women and Religion and she found a home at PSR and the community of believers that came together there.

While at PSR, Loey met two other women whose lives of faith would end up forever bound together with hers. Loey had come out as lesbian during her first year at PSR and it became clear that her call to ministry was to be as an advocate for justice. Stacy Cusulos and Jody Parsons had also self-identified as lesbian. They were all members of Mill Valley United Church of Christ. They entered the process of ordination together. As they proceeded, it was clear they would seek to be ordained—three as one. They decided, "they will either accept us all together or reject us all together. We will not be divided." They also decided that their sexual orientation would not be the focus of their triune journey. Rather, they moved through the process as a community of believers. It had never been done before in the United Church of Christ—or anywhere in the history of Christendom.

When asked questions at their ecclesiastical council, they shared in giving their responses. Reflecting on that time, she says, "Stacy was raised Greek Orthodox. When they came to a question about Jesus Christ as Lord and Savior, Stacy took it. She was amazing!" Looking back, she recalls the whole experience as "a blast." On April 2, 1978, all three women were ordained together.

As Loey reflects back on that part of her journey, she says, "We should never assume the way things are done are the way they are supposed to be done." The relationship building and solidarity that led Loey through the ordination process was only the beginning. She dedicated her life and ministry to building relationships. She did it through song and justice witness. With farm workers in California, through the Nestle boycott, protests at the Bank of America, in fields, on streets, and at shareholders' meetings, Loey organized and led others in protest.

In 1989, she was called by the United Church of Tallahassee to be their sole pastor, thus becoming the first out LGBT minister to be called as a sole pastor through the regular search and call process. She went on to serve the United Church of Christ Coordinating Center for Women and bring leadership to the LGBT coalition. As she always had before, Loey built relationships, brought people together, and nurtured gay and straight Christians to care about each other and laugh and cry together. As she says, "It is all about building relationships. Justice is always about right relationships with God, ourselves, and other people. Right relationships are reinforced everywhere in the Bible—relationships with disciples and followers of Jesus and then establishing and maintaining relationships with people (those who are like-minded and those who see the world very differently)."

Reflecting on a life of relational justice, Loey says, "The people I have come to respect as justice warriors aren't thinking about making a name for themselves. When ego gets involved, the work becomes very shallow.

When people work collectively, things get done and we hold each other accountable for the work."

She concludes, "It is the quality of the heart and mind that requires a touch of the great Spirit. This is the Spirit that moves us to do something. It is this 'something' that takes us down the road less taken . . . And that road is a lot more interesting."

Ben Guess and Loey Powell are "true lights" in the Christian faith. Their hearts burn with love and justice. They exude the spirit of God in all they say and do. The have spent their lives including others who have been excluded. Loey and Ben are not the only geniuses of justice who identified themselves as LGBTQ. Bishop Yvette Flunder and Rabbi Rachel Timoner (read chapter 4) are also in committed same-sex marriages. They bring their gifts for ministry to church and synagogue every single day.

It makes me wonder, why do so many people in the church and society find it acceptable to hate, to judge, and to cast out men and women like Ben, Loey, Yvette, and Rachel who identify themselves as LGBTQ? How and why have we turned gender identity and sexual orientation into a battleground against our sisters and brothers? What possesses us that we exclude rather than include others with whom we differ?

Sadly, faith communities have been communities of exclusion rather than inclusion. We have often done this in the name of narrow interpretations of the Bible. In an open letter to the editor published Sunday, March 29, 1998 in *The Appleton Post-Crescent*, Rev. Dr. William Sloan Coffin addressed this exclusionary train of thought and action. He wrote this open letter to Green Bay Packer football player and Baptist pastor Reggie White following his appearance before the Wisconsin legislature addressing his disdain for homosexuality.

Dear Reggie White,

I've only heard good things about you, and nobody for a moment doubts your greatness as an athlete. But if your words to the [Wisconsin] legislature this week were accurately reported, I'm troubled, and in particular about what you said about homosexuality.

I write to you as one ordained minister to another. As the Bible is the founding document of every Christian church in the world, it can't be taken seriously enough. But if you take the Bible seriously, you can't take it literally—not all of it. For instance, in the book of Leviticus, it is a "toevah"—an abomination—not only to eat bacon, sausage and ribs, it is sinful even to touch the skin of a dead pig. If you thought that insight valid today, would you be playing football?

Homosexuality is not a big issue for biblical writers. In the 66 books of Scripture (71 if you're Roman Catholic), only seven verses refer to homosexual behavior. Some time ago, I picked up a pamphlet entitled "What did Jesus say about homosexuality?" Opening it, I came across two blank pages. Closing it, I read on the back, "That's right, nothing."

St. Paul thought all men were straight. He assumed all homosexual activity was done by heterosexuals. This assumption is true as well of Old Testament writers, which means that all the Biblical passages used to flay gays and lesbians have really nothing whatsoever to say about constitutionally gay people in genuinely loving relationships.

As Christians, we don't honor the higher truth we find in Christ by ignoring truths found elsewhere. I'm impressed that the American Psychological Association does not consider homosexuality an illness, and that natural scientists have discovered homosexuality in mammals, birds and insects. Clearly, God is more comfortable with diversity than we are!

In my experience, a lot of people talk in the abstract about homosexuality being a sin, but without first-hand knowledge of gays and lesbians. Wouldn't it be better to talk "with" rather than "about" homosexuals?

I write you all this in large part because today the "gay agenda" has replaced the "communist threat" as the battering ram of reactionary politics. It grieves me to see you put your considerable muscle behind such a blunt instrument of prejudice.

We live in a land of great prejudice and you as an African American and I as a white man have had to overcome the differences, we have invented about one another. It is urgent that men and women, gays and straights, do the same, for as James Baldwin described us, "Each of us, helplessly and forever contains the other. We are a part of each other."

Bill Coffin was right. His twentieth-century truthtelling remains powerfully true in the twenty-first century. We have to find a way to overcome our differences. James Baldwin is right. "Each of us, helplessly and forever contains the other. We are a part of each other."

Inclusion matters. It is time to leave no one behind. It is time for the whole world to celebrate the gifts of the genuine genius for justice that Ben, Loey, Yvette, and Rachel bring to this world.

## Reflection to Action Questions:

1. How will you "leave no one behind" as you reach out to include all people?

2. In Ben Guess's words, how will kindness guide your steps of inclusion?

3. Loey Powell says, "It is the quality of the heart and mind that requires a touch of the great Spirit. This is the Spirit that moves us to do something." How will you improve the quality of your heart and mind to include all people?

# Chapter 12: **Moving the Needle Matters**

*We rise by lifting others.*

—Robert Ingersoll

When Rev. John Edgar was twelve years old, he got up, dressed, walked out the front door of his home, and headed to church for the first time. He was in search of meaning for his life. He was in search of God and a community of believers. He walked in the doors of the large-membership congregation, Kirkwood Methodist Church in Kirkwood, Missouri. It was then and there that he started his faith journey.

John Edgar sat in the front pew—not realizing that Christians never sit in the front pew. With eyes and heart open to new faith, he fell in love with church, with worship, and the experience of singing and praying our faith. He had grown up in a home where his neo-Marxist, atheist father had no room for God and certainly not for church. In a sense, John was rebelling, as a young man, by seeking God and going to church. In time, he would be baptized as a Christian and commit his entire life to Jesus Christ.

When John was a young teen, his family moved to Yellow Springs, Ohio and his expression of faith took a giant leap forward. The pastor of Yellow Springs Methodist Church was a man named Jack Theodore. John says, "I just wanted to be like Jack. To this day, he is still my ideal of what pastoral care looks like, as he had a pastor's heart and truly cared for the people around him." When John's family relocated to another city in his senior year, he walked out the door again and headed to the home of Rev. Theodore. He knocked on the door and asked if they had a room where he could stay to complete his high school education. The Theodores opened their home to John and he remained with them to finish his final year at Yellow Spring High School.

By the time he was eighteen, John declared his candidacy for ordained ministry. Fifty years later, John is still in love with serving as a pastor and leader. Looking back on his life, he says, "I was struck at an early age by how authentic the church was for me." Although he participated in the civil rights and anti-Viet Nam War marches and protests in college, inside he was always wondering where else he could make a difference. Where could he put his energy? Where could he leverage his abilities to make a change in this world?

John Edgar went on to be ordained and married and served congregations in Ohio—mostly in urban settings with predominantly African American congregants. But it was on the impoverished South Side of Columbus where John, in his late forties, found his greatest calling as the founding pastor of the Church for All People and the executive director of the Community Development for All People.

John loves the Church for All People. He loves talking about the amazing accomplishments of this transformational ministry. Since 2003, the Community Development for All People has distributed $25 million in free clothing and household items to more than 150,000 people. The group's organizers have helped bring $100 million to the South Side to develop affordable housing, providing livable space for more than five hundred families. They've helped make families healthier by providing fresh fruits and vegetables to nearly five hundred households every day.

Rev. Edgar is committed to distributive justice. He believes in equality of opportunity so "the least" among us are helped. He feels a deep calling to personal and social holiness. He first felt this strong urban call when he was a student at Harvard Dimity School in Cambridge, Massachusetts. It was there, as a student intern at the Church of All Nations, that he saw the congregation fully love and serve inner-city immigrants and African American people in a fully integrated ministry. They worshipped in four different languages. When he graduated, he was given a cross that he wears to this day.

John combines justice and mercy in every step of his life and ministry. He embodies God's words to the prophet Micah, "But God has already made it plain how to live, what to do, what God is looking for in men and women. It's quite simple: Do what is fair and just to your neighbor, be compassionate and loyal in your love; And don't take yourself too seriously—take God seriously" (Mic 6:8, The Message).

The balance of mercy and justice is hard work.

Mercy ministry brings us to our knees and eye to eye, hand to hand with our neighbors. When people are compassionate and loyal in loving, they want to follow Matthew 25 and house, feed, clothe, and care for their sick neighbors and visit them in prison. This is the necessary and loving work of mercy ministry. It is heartfelt and compassionate work. It is important work.

Justice is tougher to achieve. There is a fable of several people fishing one day along a riverbank. All of the sudden, they see the horrifying sight of one baby after another floating downstream in the water before them. Several ford the flowing water to save the babies. One person runs upstream. Her friends cry out, "Where are you going?" Breathless, she screams back, "I am going to find out who is throwing these babies in the water and stop them!" Justice is the upstream work of stopping the babies from being thrown in the river. It is work that goes to the source of the problem and turns the problem around.

The late Bishop Dom Herder Camera of Recife, Brazil once said, "When I feed the hungry, they call me a saint. When I demand to know why so many are hungry, they call me a communist." Mercy is caring for those afflicted by unjust systems. Justice is organizing for power with the afflicted to the change systems that oppress them and create injustice.

Another way to view this is through the lens of power and love. Rev. Dr. Martin Luther King Jr. said,

> Power without love is reckless and abusive, and love without power is sentimental and anemic. Power at its best is love implementing the demands of justice, and justice at its best is power correcting everything that stands against love.

Balancing justice and mercy, power and love is challenging.

The true genius of justice that Rev. John Edgar brings to the challenge is the simple and clear idea of moving the needle. The Community Development for All People and the Church for All People are seeking to move the needle in their corner of the world on the South Side of Columbus.

John Edgar is the like the woman who ran upstream to stop to babies from being thrown in the river. This one pastor moved onto the economically poor streets around Parsons Avenue and together with other people of faith has worked to stop the hemorrhaging of pain and suffering on the South Side of Columbus. On the surface it looks like the work of mercy. But John and others are moving the needle from mercy to justice.

In a *Columbus Dispatch* story on November 3, 2019 entitled "Two 'good books' helped Rev. John Edgar lift up the South Side," Jerrod Mogan told Edgar's story.

John Edgar said it was his faith in God and a simple approach that anyone in any community can duplicated: asset-based community development. "Change occurs when we bring the resources and the assets that already exist together and focus them on the next opportunity," he said. "And the people in any community are always the primary asset."

John said that every successful program has begun by asking community members about their hopes and dreams and assembling the resources to make them a reality. The resources are always available because we live in a divine economy of abundance, Edgar said. "God made it all. God made it good. And God made it so that there's enough for every good purpose if we simply share what's already here."

Rev. John Edgar learned about this assets-based approach the book *Building Communities from the Inside Out,* by John P. Kretzmann and John L. McKnight. It bounced around in his head for several years before he decided to test it himself. In 1999, that time came, and he opened a store unlike any other. The store carried household items and clothing, from sandals to evening gowns—all with no price tags. Everything was free, donated mostly by members of the South Side community, where the store was located.

The store was wildly popular. Donors and beneficiaries alike would mix, mingle, and get to know one another. The clients appreciated being treated like shoppers, not beggars. But despite Edgar's foundational belief that the generosity of others would keep the store flush with assets, he worried the success might be short-lived. "I thought, 'What are we going to do when everything that we've collected is gone?'" he said. "But that just never happened." For the next twenty years, donations rolled in, keeping the store stocked to this day.

Norma Hurt, eighty-five, began volunteering at the store when it opened. She said getting there and helping the customers is the first thing she thinks about in the morning. "I love them, and they love me," she said. The free store proved to Edgar that the asset-based approach worked. He was superintendent of the South Columbus District of the United Methodist Church at the time and shared the lesson of the free store with the leadership at the seventy-eight churches he oversaw. "If you give the best you have, no matter how meager it seems, God will take and multiply," he said.

From the Free Store came a desire for safe affordable housing. "If we're really serious that we want to help people achieve their dreams, then we ought to be doing something about housing," he recalled thinking.

Edgar considered the assets available—the city's South Side was riddled with vacant houses and community members in need of work. Why not put the unemployed to work fixing up the blighted houses? He preached a twenty-minute sermon and one of the folks in worship happened to be a man volunteering at the church that Sunday. He also just happened to own a blighted duplex just four blocks away. He approached Edgar after the sermon and offered his property and financial support to see the vision through. "In other words, put up or shut up," Edgar said. He accepted the offer and he facilitated the task through the nonprofit.

The results were nearly disastrous when they started—with them not really knowing what they were doing. But in time, with the right people helping them, they were able to open the place and were approved by the city of Columbus as a Community Housing Development Organization. Three years later, their modest efforts developing affordable housing caught the eye of neighboring Nationwide Children's Hospital. Together, they launched a joint housing development initiative called Healthy Homes that has built millions of dollars of safe, decent, affordable housing. This initiative has eliminated most of the blighted vacant properties while transforming the South Side into a vibrant, opportunity-rich community.

The partnership with Nationwide Children's Hospital has provided resources and expertise for Community Development for All People to establish a variety of other initiatives to move the needle on the social determinants of health. This includes working with families to turn the tide of infant mortality on the South Side. Four times a year, it holds a two-part event for new and expecting families as part of their First Birthday program. The first hour is a resource fair to teach and provide information about prenatal and infant care. The second hour is a party to celebrate the birthdays of every child in the community who has turned one. More than 500 families have gone through the program, and each has reached the first birthday milestone, Edgar said.

The group also started a social enterprise next to the church called Bikes for All People, which sells new and used bikes as primary transportation for low-income residents, repairs bikes on a sliding scale, and teaches repairs. The profits have paid for about 1,000 bicycles and bicycle helmets for local children.

In 2018, the nonprofit opened the All People's Fresh Market across the street from the church, which deals in such foods as fresh fruits and vegetables. "It invites people to a healthier lifestyle just by infusing their diets with good food," said Erin West, the nonprofits director of Healthy Eating and Living. The All People's Fresh Market distributes the most food by volume per day of all the locations in the 20 counties served by the Mid-Ohio Foodbank.

In short, John Edgar keeps moving the needle from mercy to justice. By caring for people and addressing the needs they articulate, the growing ministry on the South Side of Columbus has multiplied and blessed thousands and thousands of people.

Much more could be written. Much more could be said about my colleague and friend who keeps moving the needle. He is writing a book about it now. Stay tuned. In the meantime, listen to John as he says, "Surround yourself with really smart people and allow them to do their work. In addition, continue to ask, 'What does it look like if we incarnate Christ in the neighborhood and in the places where we work and live?' It can be small, but little by little it contributes to the greater good."

The Holy Spirit of God is alive in Columbus, Ohio, moving and caring for our South Side and the city through Rev. Edgar and the entire team in church and community development through the Church for All People. The Holy Spirit of God is moving in the neighborhood and through the people of God! You can feel the Spirit if you open yourself to the wind rushing through the city.

It all started when a twelve-year-old boy "moved the needle" in Kirkwood, Missouri in 1965, woke up, dressed, walked out his front door, and went to church for the first time. John Edgar keeps walking to church, embodying love each day. He keeps moving the needle in the place where he lives and serves God.

## Reflection to Action Questions:

1. There are distinctions made between mercy ministries and justice ministries. Can you name the distinctions? How do you get these two missions focuses of the church confused? Do you do mostly mercy mission or justice mission? Discuss this with at least one other person.

2. Rev. John Edgar is visionary and practical. He stepped out in pursuit of faith at a young age. How have you done this or encouraged this in young people?

3. John seeks to "move the needle" in his work for justice. How does he do that? Can you name ways you move the needle in your life of faith in action?

# Chapter 13: **Math Matters and the Numbers Don't Lie**

*Mathematics knows no race or geographic boundaries;*
*for mathematics, the cultural world is one country.*

—DAVID HILBERT

MATH MATTERS. OUR DAILY lives are driven by numbers. We have to reach a certain grade, attain a certain number to measure productivity and achievement, and balance the books in every business. Our age, our grade level, our value, our salary, our birthdates and social security are all about numbers.

Numbers matter. The fourth book of the Torah and Holy Scriptures is Numbers. The Qur'an is packed with numbers, too. In churches, synagogues, and mosques, numbers count. In Judaism you need ten Jews in worship to form a minyan. In Orthodox Judaism it must be ten men over the age of thirteen. Women can be counted in other traditions of the faith. The prayers of the people are heard by God more fully when the numbers are there. It has been written in Judaism, "Nine rabbis do not constitute a minyan, but ten cobblers can." In Islam, gathering to pray is considered holy and blessed. You can always pray on your own, but the power of prayer increases with the number of faithful in prayer.

In Christianity, we love big numbers in worship! We know how many seats we have and how many people are in those seats in worship each week. Believe me, Christians talk about numbers all the time. One Savior, twelve disciples, four Gospels, twenty-seven books of the New Testament—and that doesn't even include all our talk about budgets, mission offerings, membership, building repairs, dues to denominations, capital campaigns, and on and on and on.

We obsess about our numbers. One teen once told me following an annual congregational meeting, "The only things people care about is money and numbers. That is all they talked about for an hour. What about God? What about Jesus? I didn't hear anything about our faith." Ouch! The truth hurts. In Psalms we read, "Out of the mouths of babes and infants you have founded a bulwark because of your foes to silence the enemy and the avenger" (Ps 8:2).

Some of us are "good with numbers." It is always good to be good with numbers. When people are introduced in the field of finance and business, "good with numbers" is an informal stamp of approval. Conversely, when someone judges us harshly, the phrase "never good with numbers" is often embedded somewhere in the narrative.

Rev. Ralph Hodge and Rev. Charles Heyward are two geniuses of justices who are really good with numbers. Rev. Hodge and Rev. Heyward care about numbers and use them effectively in their lives and ministries. Pastor Hodge has been senior pastor of Second Baptist Church in South Richmond, Virginia since the winter of 2002. There are nine hundred members in his congregation. When he reached retirement age on April 30, 2016, Pastor Heyward stepped down as pastor of St. James Presbyterian Church (USA), James Island, South Carolina. At the time of his retirement, St. James had 1,247 members, making it the largest African American congregation anywhere in the Presbyterian Church (USA). In retirement he has returned to run his CPA firm and pursue other businesses.

One thing is clear for both men—numbers matter in the work of justice. In the course of research on any issue of injustice, the vast differences between rich and poor will come out. In birth weights and rates, infant mortality, maternal mortality, housing in relation to home ownership and rentals, neighborhood crime rates by zip codes, police arrests and shootings by zip codes, literacy, number of years and quality of education, job stability, hourly pay, incarceration rates, recidivism for crimes, every health measure from number of hospitalizations, doctor's visits, and blood pressure to mental health gaps—*all* are clearly differentiated and measured by numbers between the "haves" and the "have-nots."

If these numbers don't stagger and knock you down, brace yourself. All of these gaps between rich and poor grow exponentially when we add the differences between Black and white Americans in relation to equity, equality, and justice in our nation. In their June 2021 *Rolling Stone* article, "Reparations: What We Get Wrong about the Black-White Wealth Gap,"

Kirsten Mullin and William Darrity Jr. lay out the history of economic disparity between Blacks and whites in America—based on their earth-shaking book *From Here to Equality*.

Mullin and Darrity address ten claims that are raised as obstacles to reparations. The long-term effects of the wealth gap and the generation-to-generation effects of racial inequality are numbers that cannot be denied. Math matters. The numbers don't lie.

We need to end the gap of despair and disparity now. That is the work of justice in our society as we crunch the numbers and change the story. In *How to Be an Antiracist*, Dr. Ibram X. Kendi traces the gaps between Black and white through the lenses of assimilationists, segregationists, and antiracists. Dr. Kendi advances his vision to recognize and accept all people as human beings while looking at seventeen factors. They are: dueling consciousness, power, biology, ethnicity, body, culture, behavior, color, white, black, class, space, gender, sexuality, failure, success, and survival. In each and every case, numbers play a huge part in defining injustice and calling us to be antiracist is righting the wrongs.

Clearly race matters are deeply affected by gaps in the numbers and math gone wrong. So, let's look at how two men use math and numbers to do justice.

Rev. Ralph Steven Hodge is the son of Ralph Clemon Hodge. Pastor Hodge's father was a chemist, toxicologist, and scientist. His research led to the reduction of salmonella in the poultry industry in the early 1990s. He was a trailblazer as an African American scientist working in the federal government. He served our nation in a number of capacities with brilliance in chemistry. In his home growing up, math and science were part of the familial routines—like Scripture, and prayer and worship. This son caught his father's science bug and graduated from Howard University with a passion to be a pastor and to teach. When he graduated from Howard, Ralph Hodge's first job in Prince George County was replacing the man who had been his high school math teacher. Through the years, he has taught math, biology, and chemistry and served as the pastor of a growing congregation.

Rev. Hodge uses math to do justice. As part of the congregation-based community organization, Richmonders Involved to Strengthen our Communities (RISC) for the past fifteen years, Rev. Hodge has been involved in many campaigns for justice. In 2009, he and others in RISC won a victory by crunching the numbers and convincing the Virginia Commonwealth University Health System to change its ways and care for the poor. As Rev.

Hodge said, "In the end, morality didn't convince them. The numbers shamed them into doing the right thing."

No hospital likes to be shown its own books and how they are taking advantage of their poorest patients. But that is exactly what happened. The story is told well in "Losing Patience," by Chris Dovi in Richmond's *Style Weekly*, April 10, 2009. Dovi wrote:

> The bureaucratic red tape that mars VCU Health System's indigent program has come under fire of late. Physicians and hospitals that participate in the program and a vocal interfaith advocacy group say the program's inefficiency has a crippling effect on the uninsured.
>
> For the city's poorest residents, the university's coordinated care program is supposed to bridge a growing gap in health care. It offers indigent patients perhaps their only option when it comes to preventative care—covering regular doctor's visits to catch ailments early, especially for aging patients. Without it, often the only option is a trip to the emergency room.
>
> VCU has acknowledged there are problems and inefficiencies and promises to retool its broader indigent care program, which brings more than $104 million in federal funding to the university every year.
>
> But there are larger forces at work, critics say. The complaints about the program are varied and range from inefficiency and towering bureaucracy . . . to suggestions by some critics in the medical community that VCU intentionally holds back on the larger pot of federal money that could be doing much more good in the community.
>
> Federal regulations require the $104 million of federal money be spent within VCU's walls, but some doctors suspect that VCU has intentionally hedged on applying for a federal spending waiver that would allow the school to spread some of its wealth out into the community. It would allow hospitals and doctors not directly part of the university to create an indigent care safety net that would mean better care for more patients at a decreased cost, they say, but would also mean a smaller piece of the funding pie for VCU."

Richmonders Involved to Strengthen our Communities (RISC) saw this injustice and worked the numbers to make a change. Rev. Hodge was at the heart of the action, working the numbers to help the poor. This powerful story of math mattering and numbers not lying must be told in its entirety:

Meanwhile, another group continues its two-year campaign for improvements to the coordinated-care program, seeking more effective use of that $104 million. Richmonders Involved to Strengthen our Communities, or RISC, an interfaith advocacy organization drawing its strength from dozens of area religious congregations in the greater Richmond area, plans to call university leaders on the carpet at a massive rally April 20.

At a smaller rally last month, the advocacy group laid out its concerns both in strident biblical metaphor and well-researched statistics. The Rev. Tyrone Nelson, pastor of the historic black congregation at Sixth Mt. Zion Church in Jackson Ward, is not an animated preacher—his delivery is quiet, intense and earnest. But his words are full of fire.

"Systemic evils take years and years and years to become entrenched—our challenge is to hold those systems accountable," Nelson told a recent gathering of supporters. "It is our job every day that the church is alive to make sure we speak against . . . things that are not of the common good. We won't be quiet until we see tax dollars spent in the correct way."

Some see progress on the horizon. Pastor Ralph Hodge of Second Baptist Church on the South Side is hopeful, yet guarded. "It looks like they might be trying," says Hodge, who will have met with university officials twice in recent weeks, and who is sorely disappointed with VCU's inaction since the group first approached officials a year ago. "They didn't change a thing—nothing changed last year. I think they thought we were going to go away." The request Hodge, Nelson and RISC make is simple on its face: Find a way to use more of the $104 million toward preventative care, and the basic cost of indigent care will decrease, allowing more indigent patients to get better treatment. At a bare minimum, Hodge says, his group wonders why the university doesn't work to promote the program among indigent patients.

"VCU needs to take the lead in providing medical care—as someone receiving federal and state dollars," Hodge says. Instead, the university uses its $104 million to spend about $500 per month, per patient, says Hodge—far in excess of what it might cost simply to provide each of those 40,000 patients with a basic HMO-style plan. A recent VCU presentation confirms this: "per member, per month costs [were] $511 in 2006 for Virginia Coordinated Care for the uninsured program.

"You could almost sign them up for Trigon or Cigna and get them insurance," Hodge says. In a meeting with the university . . . in April 2008, Hodge says the university told the advocacy group that it wasn't financially feasible to promote the program to such a degree and still afford the basic care currently being provided.

Hodge is unconvinced. A similar program that serves a much larger population did exactly that. Virginia's Family Access to Medical Insurance Security program, known as FAMIS, cost the state and federal government about $169 million in 2007 to provide full insurance coverage for almost 82,500 children. When compared with the university's $104 million for 40,000 patients who mostly receive occasional services, Hodge believes the differences are stark. "When they wanted to get all the kids on the FAMIS program," he says, "that was everywhere—key chains, billboards, you couldn't get away from it." Preventative care makes sense, he says . . . as a proven cost-saving approach to any community health initiative.

"If [medical leaders] are saying it's best practice for the paying customers, why is it not best practice for the people the government is paying for?" Hodge asks. "We're not backing down from that."

Advocates may not plan to back down, but little has occurred since last April when they first approached the university. University officials promised to conduct a survey of patients to determine more effective means of providing services. To date, the survey remains in the initial planning stages, . . . with a small pilot study completed this past February.

It's even more staggering how little was done since a group of participating VCU doctors first asked university officials about applying for that federal waiver to allow the $104 million to be spent more creatively.

Eventually, following their Nehemiah Action on April 20, 2009 (mentioned above), RISC saw VCU move in the right direction. Direct action and pressure with people power moved the needle for justice. At a meeting the hospital CEO looked at Rev. Hodge with the numbers laid on the table in front of him and said, "You did my work for me. You should be working for us." In time, changes were made. The president of VCU resigned six weeks after the action. The head of the hospital system was gone within three months. Math matters and the numbers don't lie.

Pastor Charles Heyward says it simply, "Math is the perfect science. It works." He started as a certified public accountant (CPA). After years of working the numbers, Heyward was "called in the Spirit to lead people, to hold their secrets and walk in their pain." He was called to be a pastor but never to abandon his knowledge and commitment to math matters. Numbers have always mattered to him. Nothing can change that!

When I asked him about his inspiration to do justice "by the numbers," he quoted Nehemiah 5. In the middle of the fifth century BCE, Nehemiah returns to Jerusalem and finds the city of God in ruins. His people are being gouged by moneylenders who take their children when debts cannot be paid. Sisters and brothers are being violated by the rich and powerful leaders of his hometown. So, Nehemiah gathers a great assembly. He brings the elected officials, the nobles, and monied people to answer for their actions. He says, "Are you going to follow the law of God and cancel their debts or not?" He makes them answer before the great assembly. He demands justice.

This is justice by the numbers, people power bringing powerful people to their knees. Pastor Heyward, using the model of community organizing learned through the Charleston Area Justice Ministry (CAJM) as taught to them by the DART organization, uses numbers all the time. Using the model of 52/1—which means the average worship attendance for fifty-two weekends of worship should turn out once a year for justice action, Pastor Heyward gets his people to take action for justice. A leadership team has ten people who all bring three people to the Nehemiah Action. As he says, "Like Nehemiah, my colleagues and I in CAJM bring the nobles, elected officials, and powerful leaders to our meeting to be accountable for their handling of public funds and decisions for the entire community—especially the poorest and most vulnerable in the community."

He laughs and says, "Do you see how beautiful math is? I have always used math to do justice. I have also used it to build up ministry." He goes on to explain that when he arrived at St. James Presbyterian Church (USA), he had no associate pastor. With 886 people on the rolls, he needed help on the staff. He established SOOF—"Stepping Out On Faith." If they paid two dollars per month per member, they could raise the money needed to hire an associate pastor. They raised the money. But, because stewardship grew, they never touched the $56,000 they needed. They were able to use those funds for capital needs and repairs!

Pastor Heyward said at the time of his retirement, "I know the active membership, those at home, those away at school, who makes up the average attendance. Behind each number is a person I know." By the time he retired, Pastor Heyward's congregation had grown by 43.2 percent—to 1,247 members!

Since retirement, Pastor Heyward has continued to serve the church. Currently, Pastor Heyward is the president of the National Black Presbyterian Caucus (NBPC) of the Presbyterian Church (USA). The NBPC represents forty-nine thousand Black members of the predominantly white denomination. These forty-nine thousand people hold membership in 442 identifiable congregations. He says, "Of the forty-nine thousand members, only 390 are paying members. I don't want to be the president of a .0079 percent organization." He has set a goal to increase the paying membership to 10 percent or 4,900 over the next five years. "You begin by moving the 390 paying members to 1 percent or 490. Then we move to 1.5 percent or 735. Once you move to 1.5 percent, you have a foundation to put a philosophy and structure in place to get to 4,900 or 10 percent. With 10 percent or 4,900 growing from 390, you have established a powerful organization. With this 10 percent we can influence change in the denomination because all 4,900 members will be voting members. And voting changes things."

For Pastor Heyward and Pastor Hodge, math is a perfect science and each uses it to perfection. They practice justice action where faith and math work together to make change. I am so grateful for my colleagues and friends, Rev. Ralph Hodge and Pastor Charles Heyward. They have shown me—with joy and delight—that math matters and the numbers don't lie!

## Reflection to Action Questions:

1. Rev. Hodge and Rev. Heyward do the math of social justice. Are you good at math? How can you work the numbers of injustice to move the scales of justice into balance? Look at hospital spreadsheets. Are the poor equitably cared for at your area hospital(s)?

2. The city where you live will tell you a sad scarcity story. They will say they don't have enough money for low-income housing, for mental health care, for the homeless men, women, and children in your community. Do the math. Where are your tax dollars going? Is someone getting richer while the poor suffer in your community? Find out—the numbers don't lie.

3. Figure out how you and your household and other churches, synagogues, and mosques can raise funds to do justice. What does it cost to care for people? Also, what does it cost *not* to care for them? If you

don't have any way to care for the poor, gather people's dollars and resources to activate for justice in your town, city, or region.

4. Use your math skills to do justice. You figure it out. You are the one who is good at math.

# Section 5—The Outward Journey: All Kinds of Justice Doers

# Chapter 14: **The Sages**

*The sage does not hoard.*
*The more he helps others, the more he benefits himself,*
*The more he gives to others, the more he gets himself.*
*The Way of Heaven does one good but never does one harm.*
*The Way of the sage is to act but not to compete.*

—LAO TZU

AS A YOUNG CHILD, I loved going to Ethel's house. Ethel Shellenberger lived a few blocks away and was like another grandmother. I loved visiting with her. Her smile went ear to ear. Her hugs and kisses for my forehead always welcomed me. She had cookies and milk. She had a chair at her table that she "saved" for me. She listened to my stories and shared books and stories of her own. She was wise. She was faithful.

What I found out as the years went by was this—Ethel was a sage.

Ethel nurtured and raised generations of young people. She taught them faith in Christ and love of the earth given to our care by God. She was one of the greatest leaders in the history of my denomination, the United Church of Christ. But to me she was Ethel. Now I know the lessons I was learning at her kitchen table and in her garden was the wisdom of ages taught by a sage.

A sage is a wise or holy figure. A sage possesses insight or understanding beyond that of ordinary people. In myths and legends, sages serve as guardians of special knowledge, helpers or advisers to heroes, and examples of wisdom, virtue, and goodness. In the biblical faith traditions, sages guide us forward to deeper understandings of how to live in this world.

Through the ages the sages of faith have taken the proclamations of prophets and made them real. In the teachings of the sages, prophecy becomes practical. Remonstrations on faith are turned into demonstrations of faith. Through this, the sages achieve something extraordinary. While the biblical prophets are often driven close to despair by the challenge of speaking God's word to inattentive and often intransigent followers of God, the sages translate distant visions and tough messages into daily programs. What they lack in drama they achieve in action.

In his August 19, 2020 article appearing in *The Jewish Star* entitled "Why the Sage is Greater than the Prophet," rabbi Sir Jonathan Sacks writes:

> Where the prophets failed, sages succeeded. I believe that institutions like prophecy survive when they are translated from utopian ideals into practical policies. The greatness of the sages, still not fully appreciated by the world, is that guided by the visions of the prophets, they gave us the instructions for how to get from here to there.

Prophets may rage while sages instruct, translate vision, and bring others along on the journey of faith and justice action. I encountered many sages of justice in the course of this project. Throughout this book, you can find their inspiring words and stories. I count Walter Brueggemann, Simone Campbell, Susannah Heschel, Ron Luckey, Margaret Ormond, Helen Prejean, and Susan Thistlethwaite as sages. I have told their stories elsewhere but each one embodies the wisdom of sages.

In fact, Walter Brueggemann is the sage of the sages. Most of the geniuses of justice speak of his influence on their lives of faith. He is quoted and referenced more in this book than anyone else. In these "sages pages," I have lifted up John Perkins, Ruth Messinger, Tony Campolo, Marian Wright Edelman, Jeremiah Wright, David Saperstein, Otis Moss Jr., and Bobby Rush. I found myself listening to them and putting my pen down. Their words were powerful and timeless. They knew something at a deep level and were willing to share in ways that communicate with everyone and anyone.

Dr. John M. Perkins was one sage of faith who blessed my life. Along with our mutual friend, Harvey Hook, Dr. Perkins lit up my life for an hour with his powerful words and witness of faith. John Perkins is a beacon of God's light and love in this world!

John M. Perkins is a Christian minister, civil rights activist, Bible teacher, best-selling author, philosopher, and community developer. He is the founder and president emeritus of the John and Vera Mae Perkins Foundation with his wife, Vera Mae Perkins (also known as "Grandma

Perkins"). He is co-founder of the Christian Community Development Association (CCDA).

Despite being a third-grade dropout, Perkins has been recognized for his work with sixteen honorary doctorate degrees from schools including Wheaton College, Gordon College, Taylor University, Northern Seminary, and Millsaps College. He has served on the board of directors of World Vision and Prison Fellowship. He has advised and/or served on the Presidential Task Forces of five US presidents and referred to President Ronald Reagan as "my friend." He is the author of seventeen books, including the best-selling *One Blood: Parting Words to the Church on Race*.

Born in 1930 in New Hebron, Mississippi, John's mother died of pellagra when he was just seven months old. Abandoned by his father, he was raised by his grandmother and extended family, who worked as sharecroppers. In 1947, he moved away from Mississippi at the urging of his family, who worried that he might be in danger following the fatal shooting of his brother, Clyde, by a police officer. He settled in Southern California. In June 1951, Perkins married Vera Mae Buckley; earlier that year, he had been drafted into the US Armed Forces. Perkins served in Okinawa during the Korean War.

In 1957, John's son, Spencer, invited him to church and John was "born again." He dedicated his life to Jesus Christ. Shortly after, he returned to Mendenhall, Mississippi with Vera Mae and his family and opened the Voice of Calvary Bible Institute in 1964. John wasn't content with preaching and teaching only. He dedicated himself to social and economic justice, facing down the Jim Crow laws of Mississippi and other southern states, facing arrests and torture by the police in so doing. Through faith, he persevered. Throughout his life, John combined a strong evangelical faith with passion for social justice and civil rights. He has been an inspiration to tens of thousands of men and women, Black, white, and brown.

When we visited, the then ninety-one-year-old Dr. Perkins shared one word of wisdom after another. His opening words to me were, "Jesus taught us that discipleship is friendship. All of life comes down to discipleship and friendship. From him we learn that God is 'all in all' and in all." He went on to say that God's first act of creation was justice. Simply said, the creation of humanity and all the world was a just act—an act of wisdom and humility. He said, "Imagine giving the world to care of humans when you are God. What love. What trust . . . God calls us every day to confront injustice without compromising the truth and it started with the creation of the world."

Dr. Perkins continued, "When we listen creatively (which is what it really means to be a philosopher), we *hear* the text. God's plan is for good not evil; it is intended to go to the ends of the earth and be shared in all languages of the world." He added, "What is He up to? He wants us to preach incarnation. When we do, we preach the truth."

This sage of faith believes with his whole being that God is all about love. He said, "God's love is incarnational. Our incarnational God steps into our pain and suffering and washes our sins away. God doesn't get all our sins cleaned up at once because we don't confess them all right away. Once we do that, once we step into the pain and the passion, God will get us all cleaned up."

As I listened to Dr. Perkins, the truth of the gospel of Jesus Christ seemed to come alive in his speaking and sharing. He was transparent and real in every sense of the word. He said, "I have dedicated my life to the three R's—'Relocation, Reconciliation, and Redistribution.' We have to relocate when God tells us to move. We have to reconcile with God and one another—especially in the wrongs of racism and hate. We have to redistribute wealth. We have to make sure that the poor are given a chance to thrive and not just barely survive.'"

He regrets that he has not done more to bring white people along the journey of reconciliation. He also admits that he stopped trying to prove his worthiness to God through his works. Instead, he prays for salvation every day. His second to last words to me were, "I am fearful in love with God." His last words were, "Get this project done. I don't have long and I want to see what you say."

Ruth Messinger is another sage. The depth of John Perkins's Christian faith and conviction was matched by the depth of Jewish faith and conviction from Ruth Messinger. Based on Proverbs 31:1, I believe Ruth is a woman of valor—"Eshet Chayil." Now eighty years old, Ruth Messinger lives in New York City with four generations of her family in one apartment. She says, "It is a spacious apartment."

Ruth has been a political leader in New York City, a borough president of Manhattan, and in 1997, she was the Democratic nominee against incumbent mayor Rudy Giuliani. But, beyond politics, Ruth was president and CEO of American Jewish World Service for eighteen years. She has been named as one of the most influential American Jews. Currently, Ruth serves as the inaugural social justice fellow at the Jewish Theological

Seminary of America and the social justice activist in residence at the Jewish Community Center of Manhattan.

I had two conversations with Ruth. The reason I talked with her twice was because our first conversation was entirely about her amazing mother—Marjorie Weiler—a true woman of valor. For an hour on Zoom, I never heard Ruth talk about Ruth. The second conversation wasn't much different because she didn't like talking about herself. But what Ruth shared was a blessing in every way.

True sages point to others and away from themselves. Ruth is a true sage. When asked about her inspiration in life, she quoted Abraham Joshua Heschel, "In a free society, where wrongs are done, some are guilty, but all are responsible." She explained that we all have an obligation to do justice, to right the wrongs.

She gets pushback from "the young people on campus" (meaning the rabbis she teaches) about the word *obligation*. They see it as oppressive to be obliged to do something. She responds, "then the prophets were oppressive," and speaking directly to me, "then your Jesus was oppressive." She continues, "Obligation is a good thing. It means that I feel the urgent need to engage with you and respond to you and interact with you. Our society is fragile in so many ways for so many people. We need to be obliged to feel their pain, to respond to their needs, to make this world a better place. There is no obligation that's oppressive. It is liberating."

She concluded about the obligation of doing justice, "Scripture is very clear. Justice is never about completing the task. Justice knows that once an outcome is reached, it will be challenged. So, we are told, 'justice you must pursue.' It is the pursuit of justice that is the calling of every person of faith."

Even though she kept pointing to others, Ruth Messinger is a sage worth quoting. I found these words of wisdom and insight from her lips and her pen:

- It's not rebels that make trouble, but trouble that makes rebels.

- Listening is a prerequisite for action.

- Listening is a principle for living Jewishly in a globalized world.

- Listening can be an antidote to judgment. Listening matters.

- The difference between hearing and listening is paying attention.

John, a pillar of witness for Christ, and Ruth, a woman of valor in the faith of Moses, live and breathe the sagely Spirit of the God through and through.

Rabbi David Saperstein is a practical sage. He grew up in Lynbrook, New York (on Long Island), where his father Rabbi Harold Saperstein was the beloved rabbi of Temple Emanu-El for forty-eight years. His father was a leading voice in Reform Judaism and a prophetic witness for justice during the 1960s. He was active in civil rights and registered voters in the South with the Student Non-Violent Coordinating Committee (SNCC). David's mother, Marcia, was also active in social justice issues in their community. David followed closely in his father's footsteps as he too became a prophetic witness for justice throughout his long service to Reform Judaism. His influences came from Fr. Daniel Berrigan, SJ, and Albert Vorspan, a dynamic leader of Reform Judaism in the cause of social justice. As David recalls, "My life was blessed by amazing people and simply being in the right place at the right time."

This sage is gifted with more than "being in the right place at the right time." David's unique gift is his ability to bring people together to solve problems. Like Nehemiah before him, he approaches problems on a practical level. He has an extraordinary gift to address and change organizational structures, policies, and laws that hurt rather than help people. He has dedicated his life to making real-life applications that can help the most people to be safer, healthier, and more prosperous.

Rabbi Saperstein is named by every younger rabbi in my project as their inspiration for living a faith focused on God's justice. Listening to Rabbi Saperstein is like being in the classroom of a great Jewish scholar and justice strategist. Rabbi Saperstein is an American rabbi, lawyer, educator, and Jewish community leader who was appointed by President Barack Obama to serve as United States ambassador at large for international religious freedom. He previously served as the director and chief legal counsel for the Union for Reform Judaism's Religious Action Center, for more than thirty years.

He has co-chaired the Coalition to Preserve Religious Liberty, and serves on the boards of the NAACP, Common Cause, and People for the American Way. On August 28, 2008, Saperstein delivered the invocation at the Democratic National Convention's final session, before Senator Barack Obama accepted the party's nomination for president. In February 2009, he was named to President Obama's Council for Faith-Based and

Neighborhood Partnerships. In 2009, *Newsweek* named him number one on its list of "50 Influential Rabbis." In addition to everything else, he is an adjunct professor at Georgetown University Law Center.

David knows how to make positive and lasting change in this world. His working definition for justice is "making the world a better place for those who have been left out of education, health care, and opportunities to thrive in America and across the globe. Our purpose needs to be changing people, structures, policies, and laws that create systemic racism, sexism, and colonialism."

What makes Rabbi Saperstein a true sage is his commitment to real-life applications of change. He dedicates himself to building bridges and the moral responsibility of teaching our children to love and not to hate. When I asked him what made him angry, Rabbi Saperstein said, "I get angry when I see two people fall in love, create a child, and teach that child to hate. How can a relationship that begins with love end with hate?"

He continued, "Our failure to bring harmony is a failure of our will." He feels strongly that religious leaders have a moral responsibility to make a difference. He says, "We have to stop building a fence around the Torah. Instead, we need to connect Torah to life and use the wisdom gained in Torah to make a better world."

Rabbi Saperstein is able to see the whole picture of economics, interpersonal relationships, and faith. He "gets" peace and justice and works to bring them about every single day. David ended our conversation with a wonderful apocryphal tale: "When God created the universe, God left the work of justice and peace undone. It was God's gift to us to understand justice and peace. Our purpose is to complete creation and bring in a just and peaceful world. Then and only then will God's creation be complete." My prayer is that we complete creation so that God may finally find a day of sabbath rest.

Rev. Dr. Jeremiah Alvesta Wright Jr. is one of the greatest preachers and pastors of the last half century in America. Building the small congregation of Trinity United Church of Christ on the South Side of Chicago from 250 to over eight thousand members in thirty-six years of faithful service, Dr. Wright truly earned all the accolades and awards that came his way. He has been a gifted preacher, an extraordinary pastor and professor, and a visionary leader who taught and nurtured thousands of Black, brown, and white women and men pastors and religious leaders in the art of preaching, leading a congregation, and living a life of faith dedicated to social justice.

Now eighty years old and having survived a severe stroke in 2015, Dr. Wright still has fire in his bones and wisdom in his heart and soul to share with a listening world. Though he was slowed by his stroke and its after-effects, I found Jeremiah Wright still teaching, preaching, and educating me on the vastness of faith. The pastor of President Barack Obama and the man who baptized Obama and his daughters into Christian faith, Dr. Wright had the audacity of hope stirring in him as we talked. I found him to be funny, engaging, and a brilliant scholar of literature and the Bible.

He said, "The true test of a preacher and his people is tested in what happens after the benediction on Sunday morning. Does a person leave worship and enter the world unprepared to serve, or do they leave with a mission focused on justice? Timothy, our job as preachers is to get them focused on a justice mission and vision."

Sages are always referencing other people as inspirations in their lives. Jeremiah Wright does that frequently. He went on to quote Chuck Long, Martin Marty, Walter Brueggemann, and Derek Bell. Ever the teacher, ever the preacher, Jeremiah Wright said to me that these four men have guided his thinking, praying, preaching, and preparing for many years:

> Chuck Long talks about the faith stories of particular people. He dedicated his life to the particularity of faith. He talks about the Black church as the church that is committed to faith not facts. Faith grows out of our stories and the stories of other people.
>
> Martin Marty taught me that too much of church is focused on a dream world. It is focused on a fantasy world. We need to preach and teach from the real world about living in the real world.
>
> Walter Brueggemann in *Finally Comes the Poet* shows us how the poetry and song of Scripture sings to us and calls us deeply to do justice. He awakened me to this truth. Whatever Brueggemann writes is worth reading!
>
> Derek Bell talks about forces at the bottom of the well. How do we preach to the woman scrubbing clothes all day and all week long? We have to walk where laundrywomen walk. We have to talk their language. We have to read the texts through their eyes and other people's lenses.

Then he added a word from the late, great South African preacher, Rev. Dr. Allan Boesak, "Speak to people where they are. When you preach, put it in a cup of Zulu."

The sage who is Rev. Dr. Jeremiah A. Wright Jr. is graceful and truthful, humorous, and energetic despite the stroke that rocked his world seven years ago. When I asked if he had preached recently, he said, "*Yes!* I preached on Easter! What a blessing it was!"

Also on the South Side of Chicago is another sage—a former Black Panther turned politician and pastor—ongressman Rev. Dr. Bobby Lee Rush. Bobby was born in Albany, Georgia under extremely segregated and oppressive conditions in 1946. In the Great Migration, Bobby's family moved to Chicago when he was seven years old. At seventeen, he enlisted in the US Army and served honorably until 1968. Soon after, along with Fred Hampton, he co-founded the Illinois chapter of the Black Panther Party. During this time, he formed the Free Medical Clinic in Chicago and began to confront the political and police establishment.

On December 4, 1969, his best friend, Fred Hampton, was assassinated by Chicago police while he slept. It was *the* pivotal moment in twenty-three-year-old Rush's life. In time, it propelled him to engage politics within the fray of electoral politics. He lost Chicago's second ward alderman election in 1975, but won in 1983. By 1992 he was elected to the US Congress, where he has served Illinois's first district ever since. In the 2000 primary, a young Barack Obama ran against Bobby and lost. It turned out to be the only electoral loss the future president would ever experience. In 2008, Bobby suffered through a rare and near-death cancer. It shaped his life in ways that he is very open to share. He has focused his congressional work on health care, energy, fiscal concerns, and the Armed Forces. He was removed from the House floor for wearing a hoodie in honor and memory of Trayvon Martin in March 2012.

Congressman Rev. Dr. Bobby Rush is also a pastor and teacher. He is also the founding pastor of the Beloved Community Christian Church of God in Christ, in Chicago. I first met him in his pastoral role in the autumn of 2012 when we were studying together in the doctoral program at Chicago Theological Seminary. During my friendship with Bobby Rush, I have been impressed by the depth of his love and his commitment to nonviolent social change.

In our conversation, he stayed focused on love and justice. He said, "Justice is the outgrowth of love. Love is our greatest expression of heaven. In fact, I believe that justice without love is another form of sin. At the foundation of justice is love and the rhythm of love is seldom seen. It is unconditional and knows no bounds of color, gender, or race. Love is really 'kingdom come time!'"

In our conversation, Bobby was quiet and thoughtful. He was reflective. "Our lives should be designed to fight against injustice and sin. We need to battle the satanic arrangements that seek to undermine the work of God in this world. We are called to put love on the line every day."

His reflections on love didn't end here. He talked about Jesus Christ, Martin Luther King Jr., Fred Hampton, and Malcolm X as the people who have most inspired him and embodied hard-fought love in this world. I pointed out that each man was murdered at a young age. He paused and then said, "The world was threatened by the fullness of love that each of them brought to this world. The best men I have known have died living fully in love with this world. The world can't handle it."

His consistent theme of love ended with this reflection:

> I learned from the Black Panthers how to love people. During those years, I experienced Black power and love power. That really shaped my ministry—even today. My church inspires me every day. They take ownership for the ministry we do together. Sometimes it doesn't look like love to others—but it is! I think of one woman who truly inspires me. Her name is Janice. She can seem rough. But she has a heart for Christ. Every Sunday she leaves church and feeds the hungry. She has a true heart of love. Janice inspires me to love and serve the Lord. William Wilberforce, the great abolitionist of slavery, said it best: "Take the unfamiliar and make it familiar for Christ."

My Chicago South Side sages—Jeremiah and Bobby—inspire me to learn and love more fully every single day.

Rev. Dr. Anthony "Tony" Campolo has been one of my heroes since I was seventeen years old. Like Jeremiah Wright, Tony was stricken by a stroke in recent years. And like Jeremiah, Tony has valiantly battled the effects of the stroke through physical, occupational, and speech therapy. He is surrounded by a loving wife, Peggy, and a tremendous family, friends, and staff support system.

Born in February 1935, Tony Campolo is a sociologist, Baptist pastor, author, public speaker, and former spiritual advisor to President Bill Clinton. Tony is known as one of the most influential leaders of the evangelical left and has been a major proponent of progressive thought and reform within the evangelical community. He has also become a leader of the Red-Letter Christian movement, which aims to put emphasis on the teachings of Jesus. Tony has been a popular commentator on religious, political, and social issues, and has been a guest on programs such as *The Colbert Report, Nightline, Politically Incorrect,* and *The Hour.*

Tony believes in a consistent foundational "all life ethic" that has led him to oppose the termination of any life for any reason, including abortion, warfare, poverty/starvation (as caused by extreme wealth inequalities), capital punishment, and euthanasia. A popular speaker worldwide, in recent years, as white evangelicals have become more politicized and aligned with Christian nationalism and the Trump wing of the Republican Party, Tony has been ostracized by large segments of conservative evangelicalism and actually was written off as a heretic several years ago—even though he is one of the most scripturally grounded men of faith I know.

On June 8, 2015, Dr. Campolo released a statement changing his position on the issue of gay relationships, and stating that he now supported full acceptance of Christian gay couples into the church. He cited several reasons, including the institution of marriage primarily being about spiritual growth instead of procreation, what he had learned through his friendships with gay Christian couples, and past examples of exclusionary church traditions practiced "by sincere believers, but most of us now agree that they were wrong." He discussed the effects of that decision with me in our time together.

For more than forty-seven years, I have called him "Tony." That is how everyone knows him. In 1976, Tony ran for US Congress as a Democrat in Pennsylvania's fifth district. He won 40 percent of the vote—the most ever by a Democrat in the history of the district. I worked on his congressional campaign as a high school senior. He had a saying, "I will only accept fifty dollars from anyone. That way I know that not even my mother can buy me off."

Called "the positive prophet" by *Christianity Today,* Tony has always spoken truth to power. He is unafraid to say it like it is to Christians of all stripes and colors. It is this quality of love spoken to power and a consistent moral compass that has set him apart for eighty-seven years. As we talked, Tony slowly wove the story of his life for me through his halting speech. I was deeply touched by his determination and commitment to share his faith story.

He came to faith as a teen inspired by Tom Rubin, a layman who gathered teenagers together on Saturday nights to study Scripture. Tom was determined to help teens reconcile the difference between the Bible and the news. Tony took that model into his own life as a pastor. In the 1960s, his first church, Upper Merion Baptist Church, fired him because he established the Fair Housing Council and was working to find housing for Black people in Upper Merion, Pennsylvania. He heard Eastern Baptist College (now University) needed a sociology professor so he came in and taught two classes beginning in 1964—fifty-eight years later he still does some teaching as an emeritus professor. For ten years he lectured at the University of Pennsylvania to classes of two hundred to seven hundred students. He led students in their opposition to the Viet Nam War along with a rabbi and an imam. The students loved them. The faculty and administration were not so sure.

Tony tells every story with a humorous edge and every story has deep meaning as well. However, when he told the story of June 8, 2015, there was a different tone. On that day, at 10 AM, he and his son Bart were together and he pressed "Send" on a message that flew around the world on the wire services that he was supporting gay marriage. As he said, "I crossed the Rubicon with that one action. I would never be seen as a 'true' evangelical leader anymore." He was right. He was cut off from World Vision, Compassion International, and others. In his words, "People chose to be anti-gay rather than feed children worldwide who were starving from malnutrition. It breaks my heart and makes we wonder about people's real motivations."

Tony has often been a reluctant social justice warrior. He said, "My commitment to social justice issues came about because somebody confronted me and I went to Scriptures and found the answers. God gives us the answers and they always point to loving one another."

Tony Campolo finished our conversation with this reflection: "Love must always be translated into social policy. The essence of Isaiah 65:17 points us in this direction when the prophet, speaking God's word, says, 'When I make Jerusalem new again, everyone will have a good house, a good job, and good pay. The lion and the lamb shall lie down together. There will be no more war.'"

My last two sages are Dr. Marian Wright Edelman and Rev. Dr. Otis Moss II. It is appropriate that they come together since they have known each other most of their lives.

Dr. Edelman, now eighty-two years old, was born and raised in Bennettsville, South Carolina. Her father, Rev. Arthur Jerome Wright, was a Baptist minister who died of a heart attack when Marian was fourteen. After high school, Marian left Bennettsville for Spelman College in Atlanta, Georgia. She flourished, and as a result, studied overseas at Sorbonne

University, the University of Geneva in Switzerland, and in the Soviet Union.

Once back in Atlanta in 1959, she completed her senior year at Spelman and became involved in the civil rights movement. In 1960 she was arrested along with seventy-seven other students during a sit-in at segregated Atlanta restaurants. She graduated from Spelman as valedictorian. She went on to study law and enrolled at Yale Law School, where she was a John Hay Whitney fellow, and earned a degree in law in 1963.

In 1964, Marian became the first African American woman admitted to the Mississippi Bar. She began practicing law with the NAACP Legal Defense and Educational Fund's Mississippi office, working on racial justice issues connected with the civil rights movement and representing activists during the Mississippi Freedom Summer of 1964. She also helped establish the Head Start program in Mississippi while working there.

Dr. Edelman moved to Washington, DC in 1968, where she continued her justice work and contributed to organizing the Poor People's Campaign of Martin Luther King Jr. and the Southern Christian Leadership Conference. She founded the Washington Research Project, a public interest law firm, and also became interested in issues related to childhood development and children. In 1971, Dr. Edelman was elected the first Black woman on the Yale University board of trustees.

In 1973, she founded the Children's Defense Fund (CDF) as a voice for poor children, children of color, and children with disabilities. The organization has served as an advocacy and research center for children's issues, documenting the problems and possible solutions to children in need. She also became involved in several school desegregation cases and served on the board of the Child Development Group of Mississippi, which represented one of the largest Head Start programs in the country.

As leader and principal spokesperson for the CDF, Dr. Edelman worked to persuade the United States Congress to overhaul foster care, support adoption, improve child care, and protect children who are disabled, homeless, abused, or neglected. As she expresses it, "If you don't like the way the world is, you have an obligation to change it. Just do it one step at a time."

She continues to advocate youth pregnancy prevention, child care funding, prenatal care, greater parental responsibility in teaching values, and curtailing what she sees as children's exposure to the barrage of violent images transmitted by mass media. All of Dr. Edelman's books highlight the importance of children's rights.

In her 1987 book *Families in Peril: An Agenda for Social Change*, Marian stated, "As adults, we are responsible for meeting the needs of children. It is our moral obligation. We brought about their births and their lives, and they cannot fend for themselves." She also serves on the board of the New York City-based Robin Hood Foundation, a charitable organization dedicated to the elimination of poverty.

Marian Wright Edelman received the Presidential Medal of Freedom from President George W. Bush in 2000. She has been granted many honorary doctorates and other awards and published more than ten books. She has appeared in so many other books.

Dr. Edelman is one of the most distinguished and accomplished social justice warriors in American history. She has done this by seeing needs and meeting them since she was a little girl growing up in Bennettsville. She says her life was blessed from the beginning. She came to know Dr. Martin Luther King Jr. and Dr. Benjamin Mays as a young woman. Dr. Howard Zinn taught her history and Charles Merrill Jr. also influenced her life. She says:

> I was born at the intersection of "the greats"—great role models, great teachers, great preachers, great leaders. They were servant leaders who raised us up to be servant leaders, too. I feel like I have been the most privileged person in the world . . . In the Wright home, we had books before we had a second pair of shoes. We were taught, if you see a need, meet it. If you see someone who needs your help, help them. If something needs to be done, just do it. And most of all, leave the world better than you found it.

A good example of seeing and meeting a need was the need in Bennettsville for a home for the aged. There wasn't one, so with pastoral help, the Wright family opened a home for the aged—which is now called the Wright Home for the Aged.

She speaks to faith in simple and powerful ways: "Once something is started that makes a difference, carry it on. Jesus is really clear—you do what you can, when you can, where you can. Faith is about practicing faith and helping others. What you do is all that matters. It really is simple."

On children, she says, "Never give up on any child. You don't have the right to give up on a child. And never leave any child behind. Open your church doors and meet the needs of the children around you."

In the presence of Dr. Marian Wright Edelman, you become fired up to do the Wright thing. And the Wright thing is always the right thing.

My last sage in the genius of justice project is Rev. Dr. Otis Moss Jr. Now eighty-six years old, he was born and raised in LaGrange, Georgia, the fourth of five children. His grandfather, whom he knew growing up, was born into slavery in 1861. He remembers hearing slave stories as he was growing up in rural Georgia. Orphaned at sixteen, he matriculated at Morehouse College, where he earned his BA in 1956 and his MDiv in 1959. At Morehouse, Dr. Moss was taught and mentored by Dr. Benjamin Mays, who was also a mentor to Dr. Martin Luther King Jr. Dr. Moss helped lead sit-ins and other activities to protest segregation in the South. It was during this time that he became friends with Dr. Martin Luther King Jr. and his father, Rev. Martin Luther King Sr. In fact, Martin Jr. performed the wedding for Dr. Moss's second marriage. Dr. Moss would go on to serve for one year on the staff of Ebenezer Baptist Church in Atlanta with Dr. King Sr. in 1971.

In 1975, Dr. Moss became senior pastor of Olivet Institutional Baptist Church, in Cleveland, which was then the largest Black church in the state of Ohio. He led the church for thirty-three years before retiring in 2008. During his time at the church, he continued to preach around the world and influence social justice movements across the globe. He was an advisor to President Jimmy Carter and also befriended such figures as President Bill Clinton, President Barack Obama, Oprah Winfrey, and Jesse Jackson. In 1997 Moss partnered to create the Otis Moss Jr. Medical Center. He has also been repeatedly named one of America's most influential Black preachers by *Ebony* magazine.

Dr. Moss is a poet and a consummate preacher. He is grateful for his life and growing up in a family, church, and community that pursued justice and impacted lives in rural Georgia and beyond. He said, "My parents shared scars and cries as they demonstrated to me and my siblings the responsibilities and accountabilities of serving Christ and others. We received our marching orders to be involved in our time and our space and by God's grace to make a difference in the world."

Dr. Moss told me, "Every human being has an obligation to do what we can to heal this world." At Morehouse, the college's president, Dr. Benjamin Mays, regularly told the students in chapel, "Whatever you touch, leave it better than before you found it. Never let anyone say it was worse than before you found it." Vernon John would add to this, "Be ashamed to die before you have won some significant victory for humankind."

As we live in this world, God calls every single one of us to do justice. That is: we are called to give each person what is due to him or her. In so doing, we can never separate love and justice. Justice is love and truth in action.

Paraphrasing Dr. King Jr., Dr. Moss said, "Love without justice is weak sentimentality and justice without love is blatant brutality." Dr. Moss finds himself awakened in the night by the knowledge that justice is a lifelong and generation-to-generation struggle. But he doesn't allow anger to overcome him. Instead, he feels completed to be persistent in turning rage into change. However, he said, "I have always believed that the forces of injustice never sleep. The leaders of injustice sleep in shifts."

Dr. Moss told me, "Whatever takes my good name leaves me poor." Listening to Dr. Moss was like sitting at the feet of an angel of the Lord. His wisdom, his stories, and his kindness flowed freely.

He shared a story of Vernon Jordan with Governor George Wallace later in life. Wallace, an avowed racist and segregationist, saw the evil of his ways and changed late in life. From his wheelchair, he told Vernon Jordan, "I was shot and wounded for my sins. You move freely in the way of justice. I will never walk again and you will carry on. Will you consent to lean down and give me a hug?" Jordan consented, leaned down, and embraced the changed man.

Otis Moss spoke of Howard Thurman. As child, a white man pricked Howard Thurman with a pen and then said, "That didn't hurt you. You can't feel that." Dr. Moss compared this to the January 6 insurrection at the US Capitol. The insurrectionists and deniers proclaimed, "That didn't hurt you. You didn't feel that. It was a celebration. It is what lynch mobs do. They lynch the innocent and take pictures and sell them as souvenirs."

He spoke of Martin and Coretta Scott King. After their home was firebombed in Montgomery, Alabama, Coretta was as courageous and committed as her husband. She said, "We don't have time to cry. We have to rebuild this house immediately." Dr. Moss continued, "Now, they are both apart of the great cloud of witnesses."

To this day Dr. Moss is committed through and through to nonviolent direct action and civil disobedience. He says, "When we adopt the strategies of our oppressors, we become oppressors. To adopt strategies of oppressors is to reinforce our own oppression. We can never achieve moral ends by immoral means."

When I asked him about his friend Dr. King, he said he was genuine and outgoing. Dr. Moss said, "He was scholarly and yet down to earth. He was a truly out-reaching individual. He had a special sensitivity and joy in the presence of children. He radiated love with children. His passion for justice was always based in love. His involvement in the civil rights movement was not a profession, but a commitment and a calling of God's chosen path from which he could not turn back."

He remembered a moment when Abraham Joshua Heschel introduced Dr. King to his Jewish congregation. He said, "This is my friend, Martin King. He has a vision, a voice, and a way which should compel every Jew to do justice. Share his vision. Harken his voice. Follow his way."

The time with Dr. Moss was a bountiful blessing of love and grace. His sage way and wisdom were touching. His vision, his voice, and his way were compelling.

The sages of justice have so much to teach about love and justice, about transformation and power, about grace and compassion. If we listen, they will speak. If we listen, we will be changed by them. Thanks be to God for the sages who are geniuses of justice for our time and for all time.

## Reflection to Action Questions:

1. This chapter is rich with the wisdom of the sages. Go back through this chapter and use this space to write the quotes, the golden nuggets of wisdom, and the learned experience of more than 667 years of life among the eight sages. You will have super power for the work of justice and living a righteous life if you absorb 10 percent of all the wisdom distilled from the sages. Have at it!

# Chapter 15: **The Organizing Clergy**

*May God give you grace never to sell yourself short,*
*grace to risk something big for something good,*
*grace to remember that the world is too dangerous*
*for anything but truth and too small for anything but love. Amen.*

—William Sloane Coffin, A Benediction

Full disclosure—I belong to a blessed and beautiful guild known as clergy. My guild is composed of men and women; Jewish, Christian, Islamic, and every religion known to God and humanity; all races and ranges of beliefs and practices also known to God and humanity. Some are lone rangers. Some are collegial. Some are relationally gifted. Some are not. Some are great speakers and preachers. Some are not. Some are great teachers and have the gifts of pastoral care and presence. Some do not. All are gifted in multiple ways of sharing and caring. All are beautiful and blessed children of God. Together, they weave a beautiful tapestry of God's love.

There are many differences in our practices and principles of faith. But we share one thing in common—we believe in a power greater than ourselves. This higher power we serve has many names. But we believe that we are here for a reason and that a power greater than ourselves is at the center and is the essence of all life and creation.

In my beloved guild, we have a vast range of expressions, songs, prayers, practices, teachings, preaching, traditions, movements, words, and beliefs that it can cause to head to spin (not like *The Exorcist*—that was done with primitive special effects). We differ on how we speak of our higher power, but through the years, I have found solidarity across all faiths with the belief that people need to be treated right. In this guild, I have found social justice warriors. I have discovered solidarity around justice issues and causes with every imaginable and different faith tradition.

From Baptist to Buddhist to Baha'i; from Muslims to Mennonites; from Orthodox Jews to Reform Jews; from mainline Protestant Presbyterians to white evangelicals to Black Pentecostals, I have found the willingness to work together to create change in Columbus, Ohio and the United States of America.

Together, we have worked on issues of transportation, education, jobs, criminal justice reform and police accountability, mental health, neighborhood clean-up, payday lending, gambling and fighting the establishment of casinos, immigration reform, homelessness and housing for the homeless poor, and others. But here is the flavor of doing justice for all *with* all. Together we have seen the shifting of hundreds of millions of taxpayer dollars go to support people in the greatest need. Without the pressure and power of people of faith working for justice, this would never have happened.

The challenges of belief and action is something we in Columbus have addressed in our organizing efforts for many years. I am a founding pastor of BREAD (Building Responsibility Equality And Dignity), which launched in 1996. BREAD has a statement we share before each action we take together. Written primarily by Cantor Jack Chomsky (one of our geniuses of justice), it addresses who we are and how we move together:

> The BREAD organization is comprised of many different congregations, who in turn represent many different traditions. Each of our congregations believes something different—about the nature of God and the name of God. But each shares a commitment to pursue justice guided by our faith—to finding, in the things that we share, the strength that unity can bring.
>
> As we begin our gathering in prayer, we invite a member of BREAD to offer words of prayer from the stream of their faith tradition—recognizing that this may be different from our own tradition.
>
> We vow to respect each other—for the things we share, and for the ways that we are different."

This powerful statement has held us together for more than twenty-five years. It strengthens us in our similarities as well as our differences.

Organizing pastors, rabbis, imams, cantors, and more is the way people gather for power and action. As a founding pastor of BREAD, I have been on the ground floor of organizing around the DART (Direct Action Research Training) model for a long time. DART is the umbrella organization for BREAD, through which we join as thirty-one organizations to build power and win justice.

The DART model is about "Building Power and Winning Justice." DART brings diverse religious congregations together around shared values and concerns in order to effectively address and resolve community problems. However, the goal is not merely to solve specific issues. Rather, we seek to build organizations in cities that possess enough power to successfully hold political, economic and social systems accountable to acting justly.

The organizing process we use for building powerful organizations follows a basic three-step yearly process, done in a yearly cycle:

1. We listen deeply. Every year, leaders within each DART organization spend time meeting with others from their congregation in order to strengthen their relationships, discuss community problems, and establish networks. Through these conversations, common areas of concern emerge. Leaders then vote to determine a few major priorities to focus on for the immediate future.

2. We research effectively. Leaders form research committees to determine viable solutions that will resolve the problem long-term, as well as the individuals in their community who possess the authority to implement those solutions.

3. We organize and take direct action. The organizations then hold a large public meeting called a Nehemiah Action Assembly. Members from all of the congregations involved in the organization (usually thousands of supporters) gather to hear testimonies as to how these issues affect people's lives and to negotiate solutions with appropriate authorities in attendance.

This process is repeated every year, each time with greater power than before, as the organization grows and leaders develop their abilities.

Even more full disclosure—the DART clergy from twenty-eight organizations across nine states are some of the best and brightest women and men I know in ministry. They are dedicated, educated, scripturally grounded, well-focused, curious, persistent, and passionate, with a true prophetic imagination and compassion for all people. They don't get stuck in a rut of wringing their hands and crying about all that is wrong. They go out and make things happen. They understand the true and often dark underbelly of wealth and power. In the face of this, they never give up and they never give in. Most of them have a great sense of humor and delightful ways of taking on the challenges of life and ministry. They are amazing agents of transformative change.

Final and complete disclosure—of the fifty-three geniuses of justice in this project, seventeen are local pastors or priests, three are congregational rabbis, and one is a cantor. My colleagues are my heroes in the work of justice.

In his 2006 eulogy for Rev. Dr. William Sloan Coffin (aka Bill Coffin), Bill Moyers said this:

> This will surprise some of you: Not too long ago Bill told Terry Gross (on NPR's *Fresh Air* in Philadelphia) that he would rather not be known as a social activist. "The happiest moments of my life," he said, "were less in social activism than in the intimate settings of the pastor's calling—the moments when you're doing marriage counseling . . . or baptizing a baby . . . or accompanying people who have suffered loss—the moments when people tend to be most human, when they are most vulnerable."

So, he had the pastor's heart but he heeded the prophet's calling. There burned in his soul a sacred rage—that volatile mix of grief and anger and love that produced what his friend, the artist and writer Robert Shetterly, described as "a holy flame."

During my interview with him he said, 'When you see uncaring people in high places, everybody should be mad as hell. . . . If you lessen your anger at the structures of power," he said, "you lower your love for the victims of power."

Like Bill Coffin, the women and men who I believe are geniuses of justice in parish settings all have a pastor's heart but they also heed the prophet's calling.

Let me introduce you to them.

Cantor Jack Chomsky can teach a Bat Mitzvah, sing a beautiful variation of L'chah Dodi, and march on city hall to demand racial justice and police reform. Fr. Phil Egitto, in his trademark sandals, offers the Eucharist, cares for a widow in distress, and leads in mental health care for prisoners. Rev. John Edgar can preach, teach, and lead prayers and hammer nails to fix up a new apartment in his neighborhood.

Bishop Yvette Flunder can preach all around Zion, sing beautifully, care for a dying AIDS-afflicted member, and speak to the Oakland city council for justice for LGBTQ youth. Rev. Charles Heyward can balance the church budget, teach confirmation, lead the Black Caucus of the United Presbyterian Church (USA), and battle racial discrimination in policing. Rev. Ralph Hodge can take you into the waters of baptism, celebrate a loved one at their homegoing, and change the policies of the Richmond, Virginia schools to give teenage truants new hope.

Fr. Chris Hoffman can anoint the dying, inspire through his preaching and teaching, and stand strong in faith to ensure bus service to make sure those in the service industry have a way home late at night. Rev. Jefferey P. Kee can teach his Wednesday Bible study, lead services when a matriarch has passed to God's eternal care, and lead the charge on police reform in a city where homicides and police shootings of Black men have soared to the top of that sordid list across the nation. Rabbi Rick Kellner can joyfully sing the Shabbat service liturgy as his congregation grows under his heartfelt and loving leadership and take on the school board to stay strong with school mask mandates during a pandemic.

Rabbi Seth Limmer can lead classes for converts to Judaism and lead over two hundred rabbis in America's Journey for Justice, carrying the Torah scrolls and returning them to every pulpit that they came from, preaching powerfully about racial justice. Rev. Ron Luckey can celebrate the wedding of a young couple in his parish, take communion to members in nursing homes and hospitals, and join the effort to ensure inmates have state-issued photo IDs upon their release. Fr. Dan Noll can administer the seven sacraments of the Catholic Church and stand shoulder to shoulder with his friend Rev. Joe Owens in fighting for restorative justice. Rev. Joe Owens can preach powerfully to his vibrant congregation at Shiloh Baptist Church in Lexington and stand shoulder to shoulder with his friend Fr. Dan Noll to win continued funding for Mental Health Court, so that people with severe mental illness who commit minor, nonviolent crimes get treatment, not jail.

Rev. Otis Moss Jr. and his son Rev. Otis Moss III are considered two of the greatest preachers of this present generation. In Cleveland and Chicago, they are leaders, each in their own city, who everyone turns to in order to save Black lives that matter in the face of increased street and police violence.

Bishop Lafayette Scales is known and followed as one of the great teachers and preachers in Columbus and around the world, as a pastor who serves with a heart for everyone, and he leads BREAD as we convince the city council to allocate 2.1 million dollars for small business expansion through the creation of small business incubators and small business loan funds and garner an additional one-million-dollar loan in matching funds from the Episcopal Diocese of Southern Ohio. Fr. John Tapp can celebrate the Eucharist, care for the elderly in his parish, and lead the state of Florida to change the way police handle nonviolent teen offenders by diverting them to community-based programs rather than giving them criminal records—saving teens from having a record and saving Florida $4,500 per case. Rabbi Rachel Timoner loves leading daily prayers and being present with her congregation in all life-transition celebrations, and she organizes with them to combat and overcome the stifling effects of racism in Brooklyn. Bishop Donald Washington is musically gifted, one of the great preachers of the gospel, and engages everyone that he meets in seeing the world in hope-filled ways as he calls the Columbus police and the mayor's office to accountability for its "police actions" against the Black community.

Rev. Cindy Weber has created a beloved community in a church started by a reformed riverboat gambler that truly cares for its neighbors and practices radical and extravagant hospitality to all, and she stands up for her son and others in Louisville who daily face mental health challenges and associated run-ins with the law.

Rev. Jeremiah Wright, now retired after thirty-seven years as senior pastor of Trinity United Church of Christ, Chicago, had a saying in the care for his eight-thousand-plus members: "We touch every life every week at Trinity." They had one of the greatest shepherding care systems of any congregation anywhere. He nurtured young leadership that saw hundreds of women and men head for ministry during his years in Chicago. He was named as one of the top fifteen Black preachers in America by *Ebony* magazine and he fought tirelessly to bring racial justice to his city and state and our nation.

These are twenty-one vignettes of twenty-one geniuses of justice. Each one of these women and men has a "pastor's heart," or "cantor's heart," or "rabbi's heart." They get up each morning and go to bed each night with the needs, the pain, the suffering, the celebrations and joy of their community's members and friends in front of them. They are prayerful and purposeful. They have received accolades and they have been beaten down by criticism and critique when they have stood up for justice.

The father of the social gospel movement, Dr. Washington Gladden, was asked near the end of his life how he could have stood so strong for justice for so many years. He replied, "Every time I spoke out for justice, it took something out of me. But, every time I was silent, I heard the cries of those who had no one to speak for them and no one to stand for them and I was silent no more." I know this is true for each of these pastors and rabbis. I know they have been pounded by members of their congregation when they have moved to the front lines on justice action. But they heroically continue to move forward for justice—time and time again.

During our conversations, several of the congregational clergy geniuses of justice spoke about the fallout and negative feedback that comes with justice action. They also spoke of the spirit of unity and victory they share with members and the organizational "justice family" in their cities. Plus, all acknowledge that in the darkest nights, the stars shine brightest. They are assured that God is on their side. They feel the power of the Holy Spirit, the Spirit of God, the "ruach," the "hesed," the hope of standing for and with those who need us to be present with them.

Let me share a few outstanding moments in the conversations with four Catholic priests, three Protestant pastors, and one rabbi. (No, this is not the beginning of a joke . . .)

Fr. Dan Noll spoke of his rural Kentucky upbringing in a community that he lovingly referred to as "a German Catholic ghetto." Serving in the city of Lexington, Kentucky, he has built deep and meaningful relationships with Black pastors. He shared a story about when he and Rev. Joe Owens went to city hall to confront the mayor. He said, "I love everybody and I wanted to go to a 'personal place' and play the 'good old boy card.' But my brother Joe kept me honest and focused. I can't think of anyone I would rather go into a tough spot with than Joe Owens. I always want him by my side. I guess that's why our savior sent out the disciples two by two."

Rev. Dr. Cindy Weber grew up the daughter of a Southern Baptist preacher. She always loved church as a child and felt God's call at an early age to be a pastor (a role not open to women in her tradition). But she pursued her calling. She felt called to ministry in an urban setting and has spent thirty-five years at Jeff Street Baptist Church in Louisville—first as an associate pastor and then as senior pastor. She said, "I have come to see that rich and poor people understand power. Middle-class people don't understand it." She continued, "I have come to see that all of Scripture points to justice, if we (like Jesus says) 'have eyes to see it.'"

Fr. Chris Hoffman is unique among all the pastors and rabbis with whom I talked. Through his ministry he has brought four different congregations into DART. That has to be a record. As a parish priest, he knows that organizing for justice will never happen if the pastor is not on board. He is always on board. All four congregations have joined community organizing through the listening process. In his current parish, Our Lady of the Lakes Catholic Church in Deltona, Florida, one-third of his parish is Mexican and two-thirds are older, predominantly English-speaking and white. Through one-on-ones the parish is really coming together and has formed a spirit of unity in serving others. Fr. Chris is convinced that community organizing is the best thing for parish life and ministry. He speaks this simple and clear truth: "You help people get what belongs to them and give it to them." He is inspired by community organizers. He says, "We seem to fall short and organizers keep going. They keep the fight going when we lose focus. They always help us find a way to win and reach a solution. They help us discover a better way to get an issue won."

Fr. John Tapp reluctantly got involved in community organizing. He says, "It has grown on me and grown in me." He went on to explain, "I now look at the Scriptures differently. Theology shapes Scripture and I have shifted theologically. I read the passages from the margins. This challenges me to see how we are living and how we could live." Then, in words I rarely hear from a Catholic priest, Fr. John says, "As I look at the texts, in Advent and through the seasons of the church year, I ask, 'how am I being born again?' . . . The work of justice is about bringing balance to the world. It is not about getting back at someone (like we see in the lawyer's commercials). It is about assisting all people to have what they need to make it in this world. Everyone should be treated the way God intends. God wants balance in justice. We need to experience what God has created us to be. In the work of justice, we call upon the greatest part of our tradition—the coming of the kingdom of God!"

Fr. Phil Egitto grew up in Brooklyn, New York. His dad was a dentist and he always spent his days off caring for African American community members who needed dental care. He did it for free. Phil's father inspired him to love God by loving our neighbor. Fr. Phil says, "I want to be part of a community of faith that wills the good of the other and then acts on it." In Our Lady of Lourdes Catholic Church, the community prays for people under the bridges while they are under the bridges feeding them. He says, "We don't tell God what to do. We are listening and responding to what God has told us to do!" In his parish (where he has served for over twenty-five years), Fr. Phil evaluates his ministry by how many turn out for the Nehemiah Action. "If seven hundred people in my parish turn out, I get a 'C.' If eight hundred turn out, I get a 'B.' If nine hundred turn out I get an 'A.'" Like Fr. John and others in DART, Fr. Phil finds his scriptural inspiration for preaching as he reads Scriptures from the margins. "Jesus lays out his purpose in Luke 4:16ff. The Spirit of the Lord is upon him and declares and lives into the Jubilee Year. We, as his followers, are called to do the same."

Rev. Dr. Joseph "Joe" Owens grew up in rural Lebanon, Kentucky. His family had been slaves on the Porter Plantation, near Marian City. His mother was Catholic and his father was Baptist in a predominantly white Catholic area. At his family reunions growing up, there were Black, white, and Cherokee members of his family. St. Monica's was the Black Catholic Church and it was directly across the street from St. Augustine's, the white Catholic Church. When St. Monica's burned to the ground, the Black Catholics were only welcome to sit in the balcony and on the right side in the back. When Joe's Black elementary school closed when he was ten, he had to go to school with white children. It was rough and racist. Joe hated it. He was angry all the time his first year. But he made friends, including some white kids, by the time he was in eighth grade. One time when they went to the movies together, Joe was forced to sit in the balcony (as always) because he was Black. His white friends wouldn't leave him. That night in the balcony with the rats and his white friends, Joe experienced for the first time in his life what it was like to trust someone who was white. That night was a turning point for Joe. Those guys stuck together and stayed close through high school.

Joe followed God's call to ministry and never looked back. "Justice is doing the right thing—by God, by others, and by self." Joe continues, "I feel deep inside a passionate push to get people in power to the voices of those who are powerless. We have to get into their world . . . and they don't like you shedding truth and light on their lives and their actions."

Rev. Joe Owens has been one of my teachers and heroes in the work of justice for many years. I understand why Fr. Dan wants this former Catholic/Baptist kid from rural Kentucky on his side when they march on city hall. He is the real deal.

Rabbi Seth Limmer says about himself, "I was the middle child in my Jewish family growing in Westchester County, New York. I was the one who was saying, 'That's not fair.' I still say that today! The image of the scales of justice in balance is one that defines the way I saw the world. I was always fighting for balance and fairness. When I saw it wasn't happening, I would always want to be part of making it right." Rabbi Seth Limmer has organizing and fighting for justice in his bloodstream. He is brilliant and personable. He is able to gather rabbis and pastors together to create change in Chicago and across the nation. Whether for racial justice, police reform, immigration reform, or addressing the injustices of poverty, Rabbi Seth Limmer draws his strength and insights from the totality of the scriptural texts that cry out for defending the sojourning stranger, the widow, and the orphan. He also draws his inspiration from Dr. Martin Luther King Jr., Hosea Williams, Otis Moss Jr., Dorothy Baker, John Lewis, Stokely Carmichael, and Rabbis David Saperstein and Emil Hirsch. He knows civil rights history. He tells me, "One-third of the Freedom Riders were Jews." Rabbi Limmer is an inspirational leader for all people of faith. He is blessing the Reform Jewish movement, with vision, passion, and a focus for justice.

Lexington, Kentucky is more than a horse town. Lexington is packed with geniuses of justice. Rev. Dr. Ron Luckey is one of them. Ron grew up in the segregated city of Decatur, Georgia. Born in 1947, he was eight years old when Emmett Till was lynched, Rosa Parks stayed seated, and the Montgomery Boycott claimed national headlines. He remembers bathrooms, water fountains, movie theaters, and schools being segregated. The churches were segregated, too. In the spring before his school was desegregated, Ron remembers one of his teachers saying, "Ni****s are not welcome in our school. We should not come back if they are going to be here." Ron was against all the hate. He grew up thinking, "We will have to change minds and hearts one at a time." His grandfather was part of a lynching mob. A relative was Confederate General James Longstreet, one of the foremost generals of the Confederacy during the Civil War. Ron was steeped in the white culture of southern racism but truly believed, as a young Lutheran pastor, that he could change one heart at a time. He looks at that now and says, "Jesus couldn't build enough Habitat for Humanity houses to change everyone's heart and mind."

Now Rev. Luckey looks at the last twenty years of his life and celebrates the true victories of justice. He says, "The Affordable Housing Trust Fund was established in Lexington not because we changed any hearts and minds, but because we applied pressure with people power." Ron believes, "Justice is a climate that exists when all people are treated with dignity. Treat people with dignity and always keep the pressure on and always keep pushing forward. Justice is a marathon, not a sprint. We also have to answer as religious leaders as to how our economic religious system affects people. As we move forward in the work of justice, we need to do 'improv' sometimes. We have to be agile enough to change our 'asks' and adjust the 'formula' we have established in our work."

Ron believes, "Hope always shows up when our sleeves are rolled up. We cannot sit back and 'hope' change comes. We have to get out there and get busy and remember that the work we do is not 'our work' but God's work. We are just part of God's make-up." Ron also finds tremendous inspiration from people like Venita Allen. Ms. Allen has faced hard times—dropping out of school, overcoming drug and alcohol abuse. But at the Nehemiah Action in Lexington, Venita stood tall and strong and witnessed to her faith through a powerful testimony that turned the tide of an action for justice. Ron names others who have inspired him. They haven't written books or been famous. Like Venita, they have stepped up, stepped out, and spoken with courage and conviction to change the climate of injustice. They are, in Ron's words, "courageous enough to change the world."

Ron is right. Justice is a climate. The geniuses of justice I have lifted up in this chapter are climatologists. We all called to God's side to be climate change activists—in our neighborhoods and across the world.

## Reflection to Action Questions:

1. The organizing clergy are faith leaders in local congregations. Each has men, women, and children they care for each day. In addition, they take on the injustice in their community. What are inspirational words or action in this chapter that give you hope for change? How can you apply this to your faith community and your local community?

2. What will it take to move you from a place of doing nothing to changing the injustice you see in your community? How can you engage faith leaders in this effort?

3. Pick one person or one story here and contact the clergyperson who is behind that story. Call them. Email them. Text them. Talk with them.

4. Justice is a climate. How are you changing the climate in your community?

# Chapter 16: **The Influencers**

*Moses' father-in-law said, "This is no way to go about it.*
*You'll burn out, and the people right along with you.*
*This is way too much for you—you can't do this alone.*
*Now listen to me. Let me tell you how to do this*
*so that God will be in this with you."*

—EXODUS 18:17–19A, THE MESSAGE

JETHRO WAS A PRIEST of Midian and Moses' father-in-law. Although he was not one of the Hebrew people, he loved God and he understood people. He saw his son-in-law burning out as he was trying to be all things to all people. He knew he could not continue to carry the load of handling everything.

Jethro helped Moses organize the people of Israel. His instructions were simple. Moses needed to find competent leaders and people with integrity. He needed to show them how to live and what to do. He needed to teach them the rules and instructions. Then, they should be organized in units of one thousand, one hundred, fifty, and ten. Once they were organized, they would run more effectively and efficiently. Moses would make the most difficult decisions and take the toughest cases that came his way. Jethro's advice worked!

Moses was able to be the chosen leader of the chosen people. Meanwhile, Israel ran more smoothly as it developed a rising core of young strong leaders. Jethro was an organizational genius. He was an influencer. He was able to see the needs of the people, step up to the shoulder of the chosen man of God, and give sound advice that strengthened both Moses and the entire nation.

All of the geniuses of justice have the power to influence others.

Like Jethro, they are gifted at creating and guiding a vision for organization and change. There are those who are particularly gifted in guiding larger organizations. These influencers are organizational justice wizards. They multiply the work of justice as they focus on issues of national and international significance. They also gather and train state and local organizers and leaders. They influence justice policy and practices. We could never move the vision of justice forward without them. I will speak about a number of them in this chapter.

Rabbi Jonah Dov Pesner has a lot of the same organizational genius that we find in Jethro. He has the ability to see what is needed, organize strategically, and deliver effectively. Rabbi Pesner is director of the Religious Action Center of Reform Judaism, and senior vice president of the Union for Reform Judaism, based in Washington, DC. For years I have seen Jonah use his interpersonal and relational gifts, his theological savvy and his justice vision to nurture young, enthusiastic Reform rabbis and lay leaders. A successful congregational rabbi, Jonah rose to his current position because he is the right person for this position. Sometimes the best person ascends to lead. In Jonah's case that is true.

His story is not without pain. His grandparents were peasants who came to America from Russia and Poland, making his parents first-generation Americans. Grandma Fanny spoke Yiddish—not Russian or Hebrew. She remembered as a child watching her rabbi dragged through the streets to his death. When they arrived in America, they embraced Reform Judaism because it was outward-facing and embraced American society rather than looking back to the old world.

Jonah's father was the temple president and died suddenly when Jonah was young. The synagogue community surrounded his family with love and support as they grieved their loss. The rabbi took Jonah under his wing and in Jonah's words, "saved my spiritual life." His mother was raising them as a single working mother in public housing. The congregation helped his family with support for his studies at the Bronx High School of Science and a later with a trip to Israel. He was raised by "the village people" of his beloved synagogue.

Jonah remembers being disturbed by the poverty he saw as he traveled each day on public transportation to the Bronx High School of Science. Yet, it was there in a burned-out section of the Bronx that he attributes the true shaping of his faith as a justice action person. A Lutheran minister was an organizing pastor who gathered people for power in the Bronx, to do justice in the spirit of Micah 6:8. They built the Nehemiah Homes. They transformed section their corner of the world into housing for the poor. Jonah recalls, "Together, we organized and built political power for justice action."

Jonah took these organizing principles and skills learned in the Bronx to Temple Israel in Boston. There he and the members of Temple Israel became active in the Greater Boston Interfaith Organization (GBIO). Founded in 1998, GBIO is a broad-based organization that works for the public good by coalescing, training, and organizing people across religious, racial, ethnic, class, and neighborhood lines. GBIO membership consists of sixty-two dues-paying organizations in Greater Boston representing more than 107,000 individuals. GBIO organizes people and institutions at neighborhood, city, and state levels.

By engaging thousands of people in identifying important problems and using proven organizing methods to engage and develop leaders, GBIO has built and demonstrated collective strength to achieve a wide variety of goals. As times change, so too do the issues GBIO selects. With training from GBIO organizers, Jonah and his congregation had hundreds of one-on-one conversations that built relationships in his faith community and beyond.

Like Jabez in 1 Chronicles 4:9–10, Jonah has continued to enlarge his territory. As executive director of the Religious Action Center of Reform Judaism, he has organized Reform rabbis across the nation. Their goal is to win change locally as they organize nationally. Following the Exodus narrative of liberation, they believe that they are the ones who will guide their faith into the future—working to change a system that focuses on retributive justice into one that focuses on distributive and restorative justice. They seek to bring balance between the mercy ministries and the justice ministries of their congregations.

In his daily work, Rabbi Pesner is inspired by "impacted people" who come forward and share their stories. Raina Gavarra is one who has stepped up as a witness for justice and righteousness. There are many people who have done this in communities across America. Willie Baptist is another witness for justice whose leadership is, in Liz Theopharis's words, "able to see further and feel deeper than most other people."

Rev. Dr. Liz Theoharis is co-chair of The Poor People's Campaign: A National Call for Moral Revival. She works with those in half of the US population experiencing economic ruin. Every day she is shoulder to shoulder with all kinds of folks struggling for justice. There are farmworkers in Texas, moms who have had to bury their children, and fathers who have work that pays so little their family lives in cardboard boxes. Liz says, "It is not enough to curse the darkness. We need to all tap the potential and possibility that lives into the belief it doesn't have to be this way. We need to channel the pain into power and possibility. Our only true scarcity is the scarcity of our political will to fight injustice."

In the words of Ron Casanova, who has been homeless since the age of twelve: "You only get what you are organized to take. Justice is building up power that takes what is rightfully yours."

The Poor People's Campaign continues to grow under Liz and Rev. Dr. William J. Barber II. They are influencers who bring justice rolling down like waters and righteousness like a mighty stream (Amos 5:23). They continue to pressure the federal government to make good on promises of support and care for the poorest of the poor. As Liz says, "Matthew 25 is not just a message to a few disciples by a lake in Palestine. It is a message to our nation today. The homeless and hungry poor, the wrongly incarcerated, are all our neighbors, and God is watching what we do to care for them."

Rev. Dr. Starsky Wilson is a national change agent. Starsky is the CEO and president of the Children's Defense Fund (CDF), and has changed national policy through advocating for poor people's rights. Since 2020, he has been working to cast a clear vision for America's children founded in faith and hope. CDF is shaping a vision of community and our nation where all children flourish.

I have known Starsky for several years. He has the unique gifts of a pastor's heart and a powerful preacher combined with an organizational mind that is able to employ philanthropy and justice action. He always has been gifted for justice action and influencing other people. In high school, his classmates called him "Mr. President" because he had a gift to stand up and lead wisely. In the summer following his freshman year in college, he heard a sermon that woke him up. God got into him. God gave him a vision and strategy to building prophetic witness in institutional life. God pouring into him moved Starsky to form "prophetic collectives" through the years. He says, "I believe in the power of institutions to transform society. I see it in the servanthood of individuals working together to become the best tools for strategic change." This genius of justice will be shaping public policy and justice action for generations to come. I have shared so much more about Starsky in chapter 10, on racism and pain. Starsky's life story and his location in America's heartland has shaped his powerful gifts for making the world a better place.

Shifting gears a bit, I want to lift up two influencers who shape community organizations in America. Chapter 15 focused on organizing clergy. Many of the organized clergy have been trained by Rev. John Aeschbury and Rev. Robert Owens. Rev. Aeschbury is the executive director of DART—The Direct Action Research Training Center in Miami, Florida. DART is a network of thirty-one nationwide grassroots organizations that bring people together across racial, religious, and socioeconomic lines to pursue justice. Rev. Owens has been the lead organizer for one of the organizations since 1990. In Louisville, Kentucky, Robert leads CLOUT (Citizens of Louisville Organized and United Together).

DART, like GBIO in Boston, focuses on organizing people to create change. DART does this by training community leaders and professional organizers to build power and take direct action on problems facing their communities, so that all people are treated with respect and dignity that our faith traditions tell us they deserve. DART does this with four core values: 1. A belief in the scriptural story of justice; 2. A stand over and against the "cult of money"; 3. A clear belief in the power of organized people to win justice (based on Nehemiah 5); and 4. An embrace of high standards and rigorous accountability because the task of justice is so important.

By listening, researching, and finally taking action in a large public meeting called the Nehemiah Action, DART moves through the process of doing justice year in and year out. There is continual research and training that goes on. Through the power of people and prayer, justice comes rolling down!

Robert and John are geniuses of justice. They also influence large numbers of clergy and laity in church, synagogue, and mosque. They have committed their entire ministries to justice through organizing people for power.

Rev. Owens has had compassion for the poor bound to a passion for community organizing since reading Saul Alinsky many years ago. He has followed the practices and principles of Alinsky in his life and ministry for more than forty years. Although he served in community ministry following seminary, he found that they served the mercy ministry of his community but could not address the larger issues of injustice. For example, when people were struggling to pay utility bills, the community ministry was not able to address the unabated rate hikes and the injustice of this on the poor. Through DART training, and the financial support of a Catholic priest, Robert gained the tools to begin addressing the struggles of the community just east of downtown. CLOUT was born. They trained people to solve community problems and gave them the tactics and strategies they needed to become powerful advocates for change.

Robert quoted Frederick Douglass to me: "Power concedes nothing without demand. It never has and it never will." He has learned how to fight city hall. The key is to never fight alone. When the city was planning to tear down public housing, they had sticks of deodorant and proclaimed, "We don't stink. Do you?" Once when locked out of Metro Hall, which was supposedly closed due to inclement weather, CLOUT brought the media in and sang songs until the doors were opened—so they could take their concerns to the mayor. Creativity, humor, and passion drive Robert Owens. He is undaunted in his work for justice.

Rev. John Aeschbury is a brilliant organizer. He has the ability to see what is undone, and community needs that are unaddressed, and then he develops strategic approaches while building power to solve problems.

John has always been an avid reader. As a child he was reading the works of Marcus Garvey and Malcolm X. His heroes were Malcolm and Martin Luther King Jr. Although he was captivated by the civil rights movement through high school and into college, it was during a community organizing training event in Cleveland, Ohio in 1987 that he was "bit by the organizing bug." While starting as a local church pastor in Dayton, Ohio, John went onto found two congregation-based community organizations.

John is an astute theologian but admits, "I am not interested in abstractions. I believe theology must be pragmatic and relate to life. In the same way, we need to read Scripture from the margins. I always take Scripture seriously as I study the texts. I want to apply them and learn from them. I am looking for the prophetic imagination alive in the texts. How does Scripture inspire people to come up with creative ideas for problem solving?"

Like Jonah, Liz, Starsky, and Robert, John finds his inspirations in life from the those who do the work of justice on the ground and read and live into the texts "from the margins." He named Rev. Andrew Foster, Floretta Woods, Jack Bush, and Dorothy Thomas as the people who inspire him. He is always ready to listen to a new voice of prophetic imagination calling those near and far to justice on behalf of those who are left behind.

Like Jethro, Jonah, Liz, Starsky, Robert, and John have wide-reaching influence in this world. They listen, research, and take action in demonstrable ways, influencing tens of thousands of people and shifting social policy across the country. They stand with leaders and lift up the women and men who have the audacity to take on the powerful people and structures in our society. They train and strengthen them, guiding them with principles and practices that yield success. Their influence is grounded in faith and touches many lives. Social change in America has been influenced by all of them. They have all bent the moral arc of the universe toward justice.

## Reflection to Action Questions:

1. How do you organize people for power? Think about it. It may be in your local community or on a larger scale. But, how do you gather people in numbers to make a difference? If you are not doing it now, how can apply what you have learned here to begin to organize?

2. These organizers are geniuses of justice. What did you learn from them that will assist you as you influence others?

3. How do we leverage organizational power for social change? If you aren't doing it now, start doing a "power analysis" of your community and bring people together to make a difference.

# Chapter 17: **The Amplifiers**

*Small acts,*

*when multiplied by millions of people,*

*can transform the world.*

—HOWARD ZINN

IN JANUARY 2006, PASTORS, rabbis, cantors, imams, and other religious leaders from across Ohio drove through a snowstorm to gather in the center of the state at Camp Templed Hills in Belleville, Ohio. Primarily from Cleveland and Columbus, ninety leaders gathered to discern how we could work together to counter the rise of the religious right in our state.

Our relatively newly minted name was "We Believe Ohio." Our origin story was in reaction to Pastor Rod Parsley of World Harvest Church gathering over a thousand people on the grounds of *our* Ohio Statehouse in a rally for Christ in September 2005. They called themselves Patriot Pastors and "Christocrats." They were going to register voters for Jesus Christ. They were only registering "saved" Christians to turn Ohio into a Christian state. They actually proclaimed that 1,000,000 new registered voters for Jesus would "Make Ohio Great Again" (MOGA)—apparently the original test run of Donald Trump's 2016 motto. We Believe Ohio responded, "Not in our state you won't."

We Believe Ohio was an interfaith group of religious leaders that I had gathered with over three hundred leaders signed on to counteract the Patriot Pastors. We believed that our state was not for sale to fundamentalist Christians and their right-wing agenda. We believed our God had a different plan. We believed that we should be called "the repairers of the breach, the restorers of streets to live in" (Isa 58:12).

What we held sacred was the common good. According to our Holy Scripture in the Bible and Qur'an, it was crystal clear that we should care for the widow, the orphan, the immigrant, the sojourner, the lost, the least, the forgotten, the forsaken, the hungry, the homeless, the poor. We believed that the two-thousand-plus passages of the Bible pointing to care for the oppressed did not lie. We followed a God who supported the idea of liberty and justice for all—not just for right-wing baptized Christians. We were a ragtag group with strong leaders and stronger opinions—about absolutely everything.

Rev. Dr. Jennifer Butler was also a strong leader. Dr. Butler was a Presbyterian Church (USA) minister and CEO of Faith in Public Life (FPL), also a relatively new organization that had formed in 2005 in Washington, DC. Faith in Public Life was a national movement of clergy and faith leaders united in the prophetic pursuit of justice, equality, and the common good. By 2022, FPL is a network of more than fifty thousand leaders engaged in bold moral action that affirms moral values and the human dignity of all.

In January 2006, Jennifer Butler was trying to help our group figure out who we were and where we were headed. It was in the dining hall of Skipper Lodge (a building named after the camp dog), that I saw the genius of justice named Jennifer Butler go to work. Jen had worked at the United Nations and was accustomed to people speaking different languages, pointing fingers while making their cases for a better world. With her winter boots still covered in snow, Jen sat quietly as the volume rose and the kvetching (a Yiddish word for "complaining") increased. Then, when we reached our point of nearly breaking and heading home in the storm, Jen worked her magic. Quietly, thoughtfully, lovingly, she gathered all our disparate voices as one. Like a Jedi Knight, she rallied our spirit to be one and move as one.

We left Templed Hills united in our effort to turn the state around. We had a plan. We had direction. It would carry us forward for the next five years.

Fast forward to 2022. Faith in Public Life–Ohio is actively changing the social justice landscape of my state—making a difference every day in Columbus and throughout Ohio. Under the leadership of the state director, Rev. Dan Clark, FPL-Ohio is strong, growing and a valuable partner with FPL in Washington and FPL state organizations in Florida and Georgia, instituting social change across the nation. All of this wouldn't have happened if the fledgling group called We Believe Ohio had not moved forward together in the snowstorm of January 2007.

Jennifer Butler is gifted in so many ways. She is a gifted author, preacher, CEO, organizer, visionary, and fearless frontline justice warrior. She is deeply spiritual and spirited. I have seen Jen bring people together who I never thought would be in the same room, let alone grow—through her engaging and collaborative work—to work together to make change happen. Her gentle way of believing the best of every human being encourages people who seemingly could not stand each other to actually stand with each other. This is interpersonal and interorganizational genius at its best.

Growing up in Georgia, the oldest female of five children in her family, she was the first generation of white Georgians to attend Black schools taught by Black teachers in grades K–6. But her roots in Georgia go very deep. As she has discovered over her lifetime, Jen came from wealthy landowners and slave owners. In her words, "This discovery was shocking and painful. My family history and DNA have caused me spiritual damage. That spiritual damage runs deep for generations and is afflicted by a culture of white supremacy and segregation."

Butler is not the sum total of a slave-owning and white supremacist family story. She is more than DNA. She is a womanist, liberation theologian. She has been influenced by the women and men across all religions and across the entire world who fight for freedom and justice. For decades, Jennifer has put tens of thousands of religious leaders across all faith traditions and fifty-four states and territories on her shoulders and carried them forward in the movement of social change. It takes genius (and broad shoulders!) to carry that many people forward for change.

In her book *Who Stole My Bible: Reclaiming Scripture as a Handbook for Resisting Tyranny* (2020), Jennifer offers lessons from Scripture for social change. She writes in her conclusion, "God is making a way in the wilderness—and happening through the cries and footsteps of those calling for a reckoning with democracy." Jennifer Butler is pointing us forward and will not give up the fight.

In Exodus 17, Moses is in trouble. The Israelites face their first opposition while wandering in the desert. The Amalekites, a group of nomadic raiders, attack the people of Israel. Joshua leads the troops into battle while Moses, along with Aaron and Hur, watch the battle from a nearby hill.

Exodus 17:11 reads, "So it came about when Moses held his hand up, that Israel prevailed, and when he let his hand down, Amalek prevailed." Eventually, Moses becomes so weary that the only way for the Israelites to prevail is for Aaron and Hur to hold up his arms. With Aaron on one side and Hur on the other, the arms of Moses are raised and the Israelites win the day. Moses cannot make it without his trusted friends holding up his arms.

This is not an image we usually hold of Moses or of leaders in general. We see them through the heroic eyes of victory and success. We see Moses the liberator, confronting Egypt's pharaoh and negotiating the release of God's people from slavery. We see Moses the shepherd, leading the Israelites through the Sinai desert. We see Moses as the embodiment of God's miracles, stretching out his hand to part the Red Sea. We see Moses the provider, appealing to the God who delivers manna in the wilderness. We see Moses the law bringer, descending Mount Sinai with two stone tablets containing God's Ten Commandments.

But Exodus 17 reveals to us another aspect of Moses' leadership. We see Moses, the weak and worn-out leader with no strength and a reluctant willingness to accept the assistance of others. We also see his strong support. We see the importance of those who lift the arms and strengthen the voice of the leader in need of assistance and support. In the work of justice, all leaders need someone to lift their weary arms and strengthen their fading voices. In fact, every single one of us needs someone in our life who steps in and lifts us up when we are worn to the bones.

Leaders need to trust those who stand by their side. And those who stand by their side need to be strong enough and able enough to lift, carry, and support leaders. As Bob Dylan sings in "Shelter from the Storm," when you are "burned out from exhaustion, buried in the hail; Poisoned in the bushes and blown out on the trail," you need shelter from the storm.

We need leaders and we need lifters. Jennifer Butler is a leader and a lifter. She is joined in leading and lifting by her colleague at FPL-Ohio, Rev. Dan Clark.

Dan Clark describes himself as an amplifier. He is Aaron in this story. He sees himself best suited to be behind the scenes dismantling white supremacy and holding up the arms of others whose time and place is to lead us to liberation and deliver us from the broken ways of oppression, suppression, and racial hate and discrimination. He has been on a spiritual journey since we first met nine years ago. He had a heart of love and compassion as a young white evangelical. He wanted to make a difference locally and globally through serving others in great need.

He was and continues to be a voracious reader and consumer of writings from the edges. Dan reads and listens to the voices of those who have been marginalized and silenced in our society, including women, people of color, those who preach, teach, and lead around issues of internalized racism, victim blaming, and the micro and macro aggressions of misogyny, racism, and sexism. The road has been long and the guideposts have been few and far between, but he has preserved. He has listened. He has learned.

As a musician, Dan has also learned to sing in a different key. He has learned to move to backup and refrain from lead vocals. As he has become sensitized and educated, Dan has been knocked down hard by COVID-19 and struggled with long-term effects. Dan has been inspired by people close at hand whose perseverance in the face of hatred and injustice has caused him to take a deep breath and consider how he does what he does.

Rev. Dan Clark is a genius of justice because he has figured out what many white heterosexual men never figure out. God has placed him here to hold up the arms of Black transgender women; immigrants who live with the daily threat of deportation, like Edith Espinal and Miriam Vargas; LGBTQ teens and adults who have been mistreated and abused; Black mothers whose sons have been murdered on the streets of Columbus, Ohio by Columbus police, like Ms. Adrienne Hood; Jewish champions for men and women who sit on death row as they fight for individuals and the end of the death penalty in Ohio and nationwide, like Abe Bonowitz; those fighting for their lives in the face of opioids killing their family, friends, and neighbors; and all those whose voices have yet to be heard, like Minister Blyth Barnow. He speaks of Amber Evans and Reuben Castello Herrera of blessed memory, who died battling for justice for all.

Rev. Dan Clark is a lifelong learner, leader, and lifter of others. He is an amplifier.

Thanks be to God for the geniuses of justice who stand behind and lift the arms of justice warriors when they grow weary in the battle. For Aaron, Hur, Dan, and Jen—thank you, God.

## Reflection to Action Questions:

1. You may have the gift of amplifying. You might be really good at plugging in and teaching or training others to lead. How can you amplify concerns and ideas for change in your community?

2. Make a list of ways to amplify the voices of others. If you could pick out one person in your orbit who has a powerful message and voice but needs an amplifier to spread good news, how could you help them get their message out? They might be a child or an adult. Now is the time to turn on the mic and help.

# Chapter 18: **The Outliers**

*Outliers are those who have been given opportunities—and have had the strength and presence of mind to seize them.*

—MALCOLM GLADWELL, *OUTLIERS*

THE EVENING BEFORE OUR conversation, I received an email from Rob Bilott. He wondered if he was the best fit for the type of project I was doing. He wanted to be clear that he was not active in any religion or faith-based organization. While his wife and sons were practicing Catholics, he was not. He didn't want to mislead me in any way. He was giving me an out if I wanted to bail on our talk. I laughed.

In the film "Dark Waters," there is a scene where Mark Ruffalo, playing the role of Rob Bilott, is in church. Truthfully, I saw that as a sign that Rob was a "practicing" Christian. Note to self: don't rely on a Hollywood film to inform you about someone's spiritual life. I paused and thought I should call Mark Ruffalo instead. But I didn't have his number.

Instead, I responded to Rob that I wondered about that. Yet, I had felt compelled from the early days of my search in the geniuses of justice project by Rob Bilott. I felt he had a gift. I wanted to find out more about him. My intuition was right. Rob is incredibly gifted in his work for justice.

My conversation with Rob and a few other folks in my project convinced me that there are many, many "spiritual but not religious" geniuses of justice. You may be saying, "Of course there are, Tim! We already knew that!" They are men and women with an ethical code, a moral core, a philosophy of life, perhaps a thorough Marxist analysis of economic injustice or a deep-seated belief in right and wrong. Some of them loved the Justice League, Superman, Batman, and the X-Men. Some of them listened to their mothers and fathers or other sage teachers, writers, and influencers growing up and do the right thing instead of the wrong thing. Some of them are actually following the ethical statutes and dictates of their own professions. They don't turn to passages of Scripture or any religious "good book," but they do the right thing.

Washington Gladden, in his poem "Ultima Veritas," says it succinctly: "I know that right is right, that it is not good to lie; That love is better than spite, And a neighbor than a spy." There is nothing particularly biblical about this verse. It is truth simply spoken to the heart and soul of each human.

When we spoke, Rob Bilott referred to coincidences and cosmic connections that just "happened to happen" along the way. Through more than twenty years of pursuing justice for the plaintiffs in his battle against DuPont, and the process bringing a payout over $1 billion, Rob saw the way pieces fell into place. He didn't call it God (I did). However, he never denied that something was at play in the larger scheme of things.

Although my project took me largely into the world I know—the world of faith and justice—there are millions of people who do the right thing every single day because it the right thing to do. Rob Bilott is like that. What I love about Rob is that he is not afraid to break precedent. He believes that if you realize something has been done one way before, and that something is wrong, change it. He says, "Don't just follow the rules if the rules are wrong. Do it differently. Step out of your comfort zone. Use creativity in the law to bring justice."

In fact, he and his law firm of which he is a partner, Taft Stettinius & Hollister, LLP, stepped way out of their comfort zone in their case against DuPont. They did so over and over. Although Taft Stettinius & Hollister, LLP has historically been a corporate law firm whose client base is corporate America, they took the case of Wilbur Earl Tennant and then the cases of over seventy thousand class action clients. As I talked with chairman and managing partner of the firm, Tom Terp, he explained how highly unusual it was for a firm like his to take on plaintiff contingent fee cases like the case against DuPont. Tom, Rob, and the firm risked reputation and potential revenue loss by doing so. But they did it anyway, with no assurance that there would ever be any financial benefit at the end of the struggle.

Rob was not going rouge. The firm itself "did the right thing" together.

Understanding this fact is key, I think, to understand the unusual nature of the pursuit of justice by Taft Stettinius & Hollister, LLP against DuPont.

In his 2021 acceptance speech as an honorary doctor of letters at his alma mater, New College of Florida, Rob attributed this way of approaching the world as something that he was taught and was nurtured in him while a student at New College in the 1980s. They were taught to think, to gather data and information, to ask questions and delve deeper in the topics at hand. They were taught to do individual study plans on topics that were of interest to them. They were free to learn, to dig, to dive, and to grasp the challenges they encountered in education and life.

Applying these skills, Rob spent twenty years digging, reading, researching, and following "toxic bread crumbs" from the DuPont corporation to find out why cows, deer, plants, and people were getting cancer and dying from poisoned water in and around the Ohio River near Parkersburg, West Virginia. All the signs said STOP. Rob kept going. DuPont, the Environmental Protection Agency in West Virginia, and the United States government said, "There is nothing here." Rob said, "Creation and humanity are sick and dying. That is something." Rob never took "no" for an answer. He was driven to get this right. He was determined Wilbur Earl Tennant, a West Virginia farmer who had lost 150 head of cattle and who no one was listening to, would have his day in court.

There is another very important thing about Rob Bilott. Rob answers his phone (he took my call). When Wilbur Earl Tennant called Rob's law office on October 9, 1998, Rob took the call. Wilbur said he had gotten Rob's number from Rob's grandmother, Alma White. Although Rob hesitated at the beginning, now Wilbur had Rob's attention. Now, this call wasn't about cows, it was about family. Rob was listening. Rob met with Wilbur. That meeting would forever change Rob's life.

Wilbur said words to Rob that stayed with him and which are remembered in his book *Exposure*. "They wanna try and keep everything hushed up . . . But it's not gonna be covered up. Because I'm gonna bring it out in the open for people to see." Although Wilbur Tennant has since died from his cancer, he will always be remembered for his courage and determination to do the right thing.

I call Rob Bilott an outlier in my genius of justice project because he doesn't fit into a nice spiritual and religious mold. But honestly, Rob is also an outlier in the field of environmental law. He is swimming upstream to defend the earth and all of us who reside here. He may not talk to or about God. But I regularly thank God for Rob Bilott.

An outlier is a person that differs from all the other members of a particular group or set. An outlier is situated away from the main body or system. I love what geologists call outliers in the rock formations of the earth.

An outlier in geology is a young rock formation isolated among older rocks. An outlier doesn't give up or give in to the pressures of being a young rock among old rocks. An outlier thrives in the pressure.

When I think of Rob, I think of the apostle Paul in Romans 12:2: "Do not be conformed to this world, but be transformed by the renewing of your minds, so that you may discern the will of God—what is good and acceptable and perfect." Rob may not use the phrase "discern the will of God," but he is not conformed to this world. His mind and heart have been renewed. And Rob is doing what is good and acceptable and perfect on behalf the poisoned plaintiffs along the banks of the Ohio River and now throughout the country.

In talking with Tom Terp, Rob's colleague (who was played by Tim Robbins in the film *Dark Waters)*, I could see that Rob is not the only outlier in his firm. Tom said, "The decisions we made on behalf of Wilbur and his family were not difficult decisions. I have always believed that good deeds or good behavior are rewarded over the long haul. Not always in the short run, but always in the long run. I don't think of it as 'faith' in the biblical sense, but instead as a general faith in people and outcomes . . . and maybe that really is its own kind of faith in God."

Tom has always been fascinated by what motivates people to do the right thing. Doing the right thing for people should never be hard. It should come from our common humanity and love for everyone. But somehow this basic quality of life and living has gotten lost. I am glad that it lives in these two partners and an entire legal firm that stood together and stood by Wilbur and over seventy thousand plaintiffs to do the right thing. Rob and Tom give me hope every day.

Rob Bilott and Tom Terp are not the only outliers I encountered in my project. I also count Dr. Amy Acton, Terry E. "Nunnie" Green, and Marty Kress as outliers. I hesitate to use the word *outlier* in relation to faith-based beliefs and actions, because all three are people of faith. However, they are outliers in this project because they come at the questions of justice from different paths than the vast majority of the participants.

Dr. Amy Acton was selected as director of the Ohio Department of Health by Gov. Mike DeWine in February 2019. Born and raised in Youngstown, Ohio, she "lived in eighteen different places in a twelve-year period including a tent in the winter outside Youngstown," where she was being abused by her stepfather. All the abuse, abandonment, and neglect by her mother and stepfather finally forced the courts to grant custody to her father. She recalls of her father, "My dad always told me I could be in life whatever I wanted to be."

Amy graduated from Liberty High School in Youngstown and even became homecoming queen. As she said in an interview with the *Youngstown Vindicator* in August 2019, "Nobody in my high school knew what I had been through ... It's hard to tell people about this because it makes kids uncomfortable. So, you just keep it all in."

Dr. Acton emerged from a horrific childhood to become a public health wizard and medical doctor and lead Ohio through the first ten months of the COVID-19 outbreak as our state medical director. When the state stumbled into the pandemic in March 2020, Dr. Acton stood strong every day and spoke to us like we were her family. In a time of devastating economic and health crisis, we could trust her to give us hard news with an honest message of compassion and love for all Ohioans. She never wavered in her approach, even though she faced death threats to herself and her family on a regular basis. Dr. Acton is a woman of deep Jewish faith. She is one of the true heroes for our nation in the midst of COVID-19's steady assault on all of us.

All of the challenges of her early life prepared Dr. Acton for the moment through which she led Ohio in 2020. As she said to me, "In the days before the shutdown, it was strange driving downtown knowing that I knew something the general public had no idea was coming." Few of us can imagine such a burden and responsibility. Yet, she handled it all with grace and empathy. In a video chat with *Time* magazine in April 2020, she said, "I think because of the childhood I had, I'm at my best during a crisis." Her gift, created from the struggles of her early life, was a gift she shared with all of us. Amy saved thousands of lives when the pandemic swept into our state. She was *our* doctor. She cared for all of us in Ohio when we needed it most of all.

Terry Green is the youngest genius of justice in this project. Terry was raised by his grandmother and a community of people who surrounded him with love. When his best friend was killed by gun violence, his life went off the rails and he found himself homeless and then incarcerated for three and one-half years in his early twenties. Through it all, Terry never lost a vision for a better life and better world. Terry took classes while in prison, through Ohio State University, and became connected to people who believed in him. That belief, plus his own interior belief and self-confidence, has driven his determination to do good in this world.

He stays persistent and hopeful in the face of seemingly insurmountable odds. While in prison, one book changed Terry's life forever. It was James Allen's 1903 classic *As a Man Thinketh*.

Inspired by James Allen's vision of the power of thought, he started Think, Make, Live Youth. Terry explains Think, Make, Live Youth like this:

Think it—the vision you hold for your life;

Make it—apply the vision for change,

Live it—the sustaining of the vision for daily life.

As founder and CEO of Think, Make, Live Youth, Terry is a magnet for positive change among young people. He empowers them for change every day. He also has established an Annual Youth Summit and the Neighborhood Academy. In addition, early on, he was inspired by the Washington Gladden Social Justice Park in Columbus to begin and host the annual Social Justice Awards. Terry is committed to supporting youth and the larger community to make Columbus a great city for all people.

Not long ago, Terry discovered that he was a cousin of Emmett Till. When we talked, he said, "It is in my DNA to do social justice. My cousin inspires me to do justice." Terry, your cousin inspires me to do justice, too. So do you.

Marty Kress was inspired by a Catholic education and faith to make a difference in our world in wonderful ways. In his words, "I think I have more education in Catholic institutes than most priests—kindergarten to high school (thirteen years), Notre Dame (four years), Georgetown (three years), Catholic University (one year)."

I love what Marty said next, "But—and this a big 'but'—the different social and community activities I have supported were not driven by Scripture or biblically grounded justice ministries as a few of your questions imply. Rather, they were driven by my value system, my education, family, life experiences, dreams and aspirations, channeling my 'inner Marty' or conscience."

Thank you, Marty. How many people in this world can relate to an inner voice or conscience guiding them? I believe all of us can relate to Marty on this. I remember watching *Pinocchio* as a child and thinking, "That little bug Jiminy Cricket lives inside of me, too."

Attending Notre Dame when Fr. Theodore Hesburgh was president, Marty was inspired to make a difference in the world. Fr. Hesburgh always encouraged the Notre Dame students to go out in the world and be change agents. Marty embodies this quote from Fr. Hesburgh: "The very essence of leadership is that you have to have vision. You can't blow an uncertain trumpet." While in college, Marty helped children in the inner city of South Bend. When he went out to work after college, he lived by the adage, "A job feeds you and your family. Volunteer work gives meaning to your life." This inspired Marty to volunteer as the fund distribution co-chair for the United Way, chair the Buckeye Regional Robotics Competition, serve on an Advisory Committee at Central State, and stand up for the Global Water Institute at Ohio State.

Whether in the Marines during the Viet Nam War era, or as deputy director for the NASA Glenn Research Center, or later in life working with Ohio State University to provide clean water to rural Africans, Marty is a person who sees a problem and solves it. He says today, "I always had mentors in my life who helped develop me. They always pushed me to have a wider vision and meet the world's needs in the work that I did."

Rob, Tom, Amy, Terry, and Marty are geniuses of justice. They have qualities of fairness and kindness, courage and tenacity, vision and hope, wisdom, and a deep sense of doing the right thing for those in need. I am tempted to use God talk to talk about my friends. But they have their own words to say what they are doing and they step into it every day to make a difference in this world. I love that about these five special people.

I call them my outliers in the genius of justice project. But truthfully, they are not outliers at all. They each have a following of people who find them inspiring and attractive as leaders. I think of them as like the Justice League of America in DC Comics. They are superheroes who we all want to follow. They get things done. They stick with their vision of a better world and see it through. Make no mistake about it, they are worthy heroes in a project filled with exceptional people.

I have always been inspired by outliers. I am sure you have been inspired by outliers, too. One of my favorite outliers in Holy Scripture is Mary Magdalene. In the beautiful film *Mary Magdalene*, released in 2018, we come to know a compassionate Mary. Though she is silent through most of the film, after seeing our risen Savior, she comes and tells the disciples, "I have seen the Lord." As the film ends, she teaches them the true meaning of Jesus' life and resurrection.

> This whole time we have been looking for a change in the world but it's not what we thought. The kingdom is here now. It's not something we can see with our eyes. It's here within us. All we

have to do is let go of our anguish and our resentment and become like children—just as he said. The kingdom can't be built through conflict—not by opposition, not by destruction. It grows with us with every act of love and care, with our forgiveness. We have the power to lift the people—just as he did. Then we will be free—just as he is. We have the power to relieve the suffering of the poor. It is up to us. The world will only change as we change. I will not stay and be silent. I will be heard.

Like Mary Magdalene and so many powerful and just outliers in this world, Rob, Tom, Amy, Terry, and Marty will not stay silent. They will be heard. I am listening. I hope you are listening too.

### Reflection to Action Questions:

1. Are you an outlier? Do you know anyone who is? They are conditioned to do good. They are wired for compassionate care. They come to this naturally. List the "outliers" in your life who inspire you to do the right thing.

2. Who are your heroes outside faith communities (and there may be a ton of them)? Write down the things you have learned from them to be a difference-maker in this world.

# Chapter 19: "The Others" Must Be Seen and Felt

*The reason why we hate one another or fear one another is*
*that we secretly, or openly, hate and fear our own selves.*

—THOMAS MERTON

IT WAS LATE ON a chilly autumn evening when I met Power at church. Unlike others who come late at night, Power's request was different. He did not ask for money or any help of any kind. He simply wanted me to call the police.

He was sleeping under the shelter of our Broad Street entrance—next to the front doors, beneath the chiseled words, "Enter to Worship, Depart to Serve." He asked if I could tell the police that it was okay for him to sleep there. I agreed to call them. Although I offered him food and drink and blankets, he politely declined. Instead, he asked what time he could return in the morning to work for the church. He desired to work as a thanksgiving to us for our kindness, not for pay. I said, "Okay," and continued, "Power, why our front steps? Why in the floodlights and noise of Broad Street?" He answered, "I feel safe in the light. I feel safe in the shelter of God's house."

The next morning, Power arrived early to begin caring for First Church. On his first day of work, Power raked up twenty-two bags of leaves in ninety minutes. When a member bought a pair of gloves for Power to protect his hands from the cold, he returned them, encouraging us to give them to someone who was really in need. Having been abused and even shot in the stomach by his cocaine-addicted father at thirteen, Power hated to be touched and trusted very few people. In the weeks that followed, it became clear that even the floodlights and shelter of our cathedral stone could not provide what he really needed. Yet, he declined homeless shelters and even offers of other housing. One night, carrying his graceful yet troubled life and his servant spirit with him, Power disappeared onto the streets of Columbus.

I think of Power often. Bathed in the light and sheltered by God, my abolitionist congregation has sought for 170 years to minister to the Powers in the heart of the city. Although the mason's chisel has whittled in stone a command to worship and serve, we have, at times, fallen short of both worship and service. Nevertheless, God has blessed us through the years with Power and other men and women like Power who call us to ways of justice and mercy.

When Power first approached me, I did not see the man he was. I did not receive him as a friend on the journey of life. I saw him for the transaction I assumed was about to happen. I braced for "the ask" without seeing the person standing in front of me. The essence of the man was first lost to me. He was the one who broke the icy wall I put up as shield. In his own brokenness, Power was more vulnerable and honest than I.

Too many of us do not know how to love. How are we going to recover the ability to love ourselves and to love one another? Thomas Merton, writing in *The Living Bread*, put it this way:

> The reason why we hate one another or fear one another is that we secretly, or openly, hate and fear our own selves. And we hate ourselves because the depths of our being are a chaos of frustration and spiritual misery. Lonely and helpless, we cannot be at peace with others because we are not at peace with ourselves, and we cannot be at peace with ourselves because we are not at peace with God.

Throughout my project, people would talk about "the Others." Sometimes they would speak of "Othering." Like Power, "the Others" sleep on the steps of my church at night. They are frightened to go inside shelters and transitional housing. They are children who have dropped out of school and "disappeared" in the pandemic. They are women who work three jobs and still can't find a place to call home for their children. "The Others" are nameless and faceless to too many of us. And yet, their very presence in my life and in our world motivates me every day to get up and fight for justice. They must be named. Their faces must be seen and known. They must not be forgotten or forsaken. They are, in the words of Scripture, "the poor who are with us always."

I see "the Others" as the fifty-fourth genius of justice.

Having said this, I know "the Other" can be a complex concept. In one sense, everyone is "the Other" to us and we are "the Other" to everyone else. In this way, "the Other" is always changing and always elusive.

When I speak of "the Other," I mean the ones who have been left behind in the economy of our nation and world. They have been denied power or stripped of power. They are "them" to the power brokers—who always identify themselves as "us." In the classic axes of discrimination and power differences, "the Others" are too easily cast aside by classifications of age, sexuality, gender identity, immigration status, ethnicity, race, caste, income, and class.

The true genius of justice is to know their names. The nameless multitudes become known each by their name and their life story. Relationships develop and hope becomes embodied. When this happens, "the Others" are no longer set apart from our lives. Rather, they become important parts of our lives. This becomes so apparent that "they" are now "we." "Those people" become "our people." This is a key to organizing for justice.

I witnessed the genius of "the Others" during the annual assembly of BREAD (Building Responsibility Equality And Dignity) on November 12, 2012, at Christ the King Catholic Church in Columbus, Ohio. That night, I experienced a conversion of heart. I saw what love looks like in action!

Here is what happened: We were all gathered for the annual assembly trying to figure out what issue to tackle in 2013. Each problem and an accompanying testimonial were presented. The issues were crime and violence, education, and discrimination against immigrants. Through the years, I have listened to these kinds of presentations, presentations on public education, street violence, crime and drugs, fair housing, public transportation, jobs, health care, youth and the criminal justice system, and more.

All of the issues are worthy of our time and efforts. Sometimes I have found these presentations touching and sometimes tedious. But I have always tried to listen. On this night, as the issue on discrimination against immigrants was presented, I listened to our speaker in Spanish and English. It was powerful as the witness told a story about their encounter with injustice as an immigrant coming into Columbus. My mind drifted back to my ancestors facing various degrees of hardship and peril upon arrival in this new land—a land full of hope and dreams for immigrants from Europe, Asia, and Latin America, and a land full of slavery and pain for African American brothers and sisters coming to our shores.

When the vote was taken, a block of seventy-five mostly Latina members of Christ the King Church voted for the discrimination issue as a focus. Never had that happened in seventeen years of BREAD doing justice in this city. The room was stunned. The issue won the night. As the meeting concluded and people dispersed to their cars and homes, I made my way to the Christ the King delegation. Through a translator, I thanked the group for hosting us and for their courage to come out, speak out, and vote for this issue.

That is when the conversion happened.

This mostly poor, and mostly brown-skinned group of Christians clapped and danced, cried and smiled. They embraced me and thanked me for my kindness. Quite frankly, I was "the Other" to them. And yet, we became family to one another as they welcomed me and loved me for my words of thanks. Then one man, with clear and loving eyes, asked me to pray for them. We all held hands and through a translator, I led the prayers, ending with the Lord's Prayer. As I offered the prayer, I felt my arms rising as the words of our Savior enveloped the room in Spanish and hands were raised as one.

When the prayer closed and my eyes opened, I glanced upon an image of Christ by the altar with his hands raised. I saw his face. Then, I looked around the circle and found myself falling in love. I saw eyes of love all around me. My heart had been warmed by the love of God. I was converted to my own faith by people who spoke God's name in another language in my own city. BREAD had risen.

Bishop Lafayette Scales, founder and pastor of Rhema Christian Center, and one of the geniuses of justice, told a story years ago of William Booth, founder of the Salvation Army. It was Christmastime and Booth was trying to get a telegraph out for a Christmas message to his loyal Salvation Army workers. He had very little money. He kept offering words to the telegraph office worker. The man kept saying, to him, you do not have enough money to send this. Finally, after three attempts, Booth wrote one word and handed it to the young man. The word was *others*.

Love "the Others."

As you love "the Others," you will come to know a love and peace within your own heart and soul. As you love "the Others," the work of justice will reveal itself in new and beautiful ways.

## Reflection to Action Questions:

1. Have you ever felt like "the Other" or part of a group of "them"? How has that felt to you? How has it affected you?

2. Have you witnessed the "Othering" of people in your school, your neighborhood, your town or city? What have you done about it?

3. Write down five ways you can reach and positively impact the lives of those who are "the Other" in your community and bring them into your circle of love.

# Section 6—**Moving Forward: The Drumbeat of Justice**

# Chapter 20: **You Be the Justice You Want to See**

*Justice is what love looks like in public.*

—CORNEL WEST

As WE COME TO the end of this book, it is clear that justice does not just happen. It consists of the collective, collaborative, faith-based, and people power-based efforts that ultimately bend the moral arc of the universe. And we know the moral arc of the universe will never bend itself. It takes all kinds of different people working together to bend the arc, often in small and incremental ways.

In the book of Nehemiah, the walls around the city of Jerusalem are rebuilt in fifty-two days. Nehemiah gathers and trains all the people to work on their part of the wall. It takes all the people working together, on separate sections of the wall, to complete the entire process. That is what a plan for justice action often looks like. It is sweeping in nature but breaks down into specific sections. In the book of Nehemiah, the prophet presents us with such a plan.

Here are ten principles drawn from Nehemiah that guide us to justice action:

1. We listen to beloved friends who speak the truth about the place we love (1:2–3).

2. We confess our brokenness and pray continuously for God's strength and leadership (1:4–11).

3. We risk being honest and live with the results (2:1–10).

4. We believe God's plans are simple, specific, and impossible (2:17).

5. We trust in the Holy Spirit to spark the visionary leadership of the congregation (2:18ff).

6. We build a broad base upon a solid foundation (3:28–4:9).

7. We confront injustice when we meet it as leaders and as congregations, thus dealing with disheartening lags in the building process (5:1–19).

8. We celebrate our victories with great joy while living faithfully in God's Word (7:73b–8:18).

9. We move forward in faith—always aware of the potentially destructive opposition that arises in the rebuilding process (6:1–16).

10. We continue to risk for health and growth (13:5–9).

As we do justice, we must figure out ways to bring our justice action into focus. Social justice has many faces. As Walter Brueggemann says, "Justice is the work of figuring what was taken from whom and returning it to them." Like a kaleidoscope, justice may look different at different times and be examined from different angles. For example, years ago, Washington Gladden fought for "pure milk" for children. I always thought this was about pasteurized milk. But there was a time, at the turn of the last century, when bottling companies were dumping watered-down milk with white paint mixed in to impoverished communities. Greed and the lack of any more regulations that protected people from this form of food poisoning were addressed by the Pure Milk Crusade. The Pure Milk Crusade was an actual justice action to stop this poisoning of the poor.

That is the work of social justice. It can be large or small. But it must be.

My congregation, First Congregational Church United Church of Christ in Columbus, Ohio, believes so much in social justice that we built the first social justice park in America. Named the Washington Gladden Social Justice Park, it is the people's park. Small, but mighty, it stands on the corner of Cleveland Avenue and Broad Street in downtown Columbus. Built on the land of First Congregational Church United Church of Christ, and with the cooperation of civic leaders, philanthropists, and government investments, the park opened in October 2018. The park features gardens and trees, a pathway of justice, a wall of honor, and a public sculpture called "A Single Garment of Destiny," based on Rev. Dr. Martin Luther King Jr.'s words:

> We must all learn to live together as brothers or we will all perish together as fools. We are tied together in the single garment of destiny, caught in an inescapable network of mutuality. And whatever affects one directly affects all indirectly. For some strange reason I can never be what I ought to be until you are

what you ought to be. This is the way God's universe is made; this is the way it is structured.

The pathway of justice winds like a river through the park. In the pathway, sixty bluestones silently speak their messages of love and justice. Bearing quotes from sacred texts and justice warriors throughout time, currently thirty-seven stones adorn the pathway, awaiting twenty-three further stones with messages of justice witness.

The thirty-seven stones lift up the Abrahamic faith traditions with words from Leviticus and Micah, two quotes from Matthew, and one from the Prophet Mohammed. But there is so much more. There are quotes from Mahatma Gandhi, Denny Griffith, Theodore Parker, Dorothy Day, A. Phillip Randolph, Michelle Alexander, Harvey Milk, Dr. Seuss, Martin Luther King Jr., Jose Rodriquez, Maya Angelou, Bill Willis Sr., Howard Thurman, Timothy Ahrens, Toni Morrison, Desmond Tutu, Michelle Obama, Audre Lorde, Washington Gladden, Catherine of Siena, Eleanor Roosevelt, Tatanka Iyotanka (known as Sitting Bull), Miriam Therese Winter, Laurence Overmire, Jane Addams, Aminah Robinson, Toni Morrison, Amanda Gorman, Ruth Bader Ginsburg, James Poindexter, Marian Wright Edelman, and Margaret Mead. The pathway of justice represents a path of learning, a path of hope, a path of diversity, a path of interfaith action, and a path of inspiration. Nowhere else in the world will you find such a diverse pathway of justice witness.

The park stands as a tribute to Washington Gladden, who was pastor of First Congregational Church, Columbus, from 1882 to 1918. Walter Rauschenbusch called Washington Gladden "the Father of the Social Gospel Movement." Gladden was a man who was unafraid to speak the truth with love. While some would say the church has no role to play on issues dealing with social justice, Gladden believed the opposite. He believed the church should be in the center of justice action. He believed salvation was personal and social. As LaFayette Scales asks, "What good is a great church in a failing neighborhood?"

When addressing labor questions in the early part of the twentieth century, Gladden said:

> The labor question is in part an economic question, and all economic questions are fundamentally religious questions. [In fact], there are no purely spiritual interests, since spiritual forces all incarnate themselves in the facts of every-day life, and can only be known as they are there manifested. . . . There is indeed danger

that the Church will make mistakes in dealing with such questions, but that the greatest of all mistakes is in ignoring them. . . . There are no souls that are more in need of saving than the souls getting entangled in the materialisms that undervalue manhood; and there are no people who need moral guidance more than those who are grappling with the manifold phases of the labor question.

The time has come for you to figure out what you will do for social justice. How will you stand up and make a difference?

As a young man, I heard theologian Robert McAfee Brown of Union Seminary in New York present three guidelines for determining prophetic witness. He was speaking at a forum at Macalester College five years after the Viet Nam War. Dr. Brown implored us as young people to be aware that we were privileged and educated men and women. But what we did with the education and privileges could make a world of difference.

Dr. Brown said: "Stand up and speak out on behalf of the poor and those who need your voice in this world. Remember that:

1. Where you stand will determine what you see.

2. Whom you stand with will determine what you hear.

3. And what you see and hear will determine what you say and what you do."

Where will you stand? With whom will you stand? Once you have stood with those who have previously been out of your sight and listened to their powerful testimonies of truth, you will never go back to the place from whence you came. Once you have been forever changed, your love will deepen and you will be on your own pathway of justice, winding your way through a lifetime of prayer and action.

As you have learned from and been inspired by the geniuses of justice, you have gained insights into the essence of social justice. You know the ground on which we stand for justice includes biblical knowledge and prophetic imagination. You know to be attentive to the influence of generation-to-generation empowering change—and when there is no one in your family story, adopt someone and become the first generation of justice-doers. You know that someone living close to you is "doing the right thing." Find them and work together with them. They will become like family to you.

You know there is an inward journey of justice. You know cold anger fuels change over the rage that flies all over the place in our times. You know that listening deeply in a spirit of love leads to social change. You know that you need to pray and meditate like you mean it. Do not get caught up in your lack of listening or your lack of praying. Instead, change your ways so that you may be, in St. Francis's words, "an instrument of change."

You know that gates have been closed to keep out the poor in our midst and lock in the rich. Open the gates! You know that people have been incarcerated and condemned to death and our society has "thrown away the keys" and counted them dead and gone. Raise the dead!

You know what matters. You know that racism and pain have separated us falsely. Be human. See and interact with others who are different than you, acknowledging their pain and supporting them in their humanity. You know that we have excluded far too many for far too long because of their different sexual orientation and gender identity. Learn to deal with your own issues around others' differences. Leave no behind because together we will change this broken world for better. You know moving the needle matters. Move the needle a little each day. You know numbers matters—so do the math and count the numbers. Add people who are crying in need to each of your equations of love and justice.

You know there is an outward journey of justice. On this part of the journey, you will encounter sages, wise women and men who have laid down their lives for what is right and just. They are our inspiration and our teachers. Listen to them so that you may embody their wisdom in your life.

You know there are organized pastors, priests, rabbis, cantors, and imams on this journey who are powerful leaders in the work of justice. They are in churches, synagogues, and mosques close to you. Find out who they are and listen to them, learn from them, and join them in the battle for justice. You know there are influencers on this journey. They are organizational justice wizards who have hearts, minds, and organizational expertise to push and pull toward a larger, more glorious vision for a better world. You know there are amplifiers on this justice journey. They will give help you find your voice and train you to lift it up in this glorious work for justice. You know there are outliers on this journey. They are remarkable men and women who "do the right thing." They have an inner compass that is not necessarily faith-based but is a moral code and a vision for a better world. They are the Justice League!

You also know there are the tens of millions of "the Others," who must be seen and heard and felt. "The Others" are walking right beside us. Do you see them? Do you know their names and their stories? They can no longer be nameless and faceless to you. They must never be forgotten or forsaken. "The Others" are the fifty-fourth genius of justice.

And you are the fifty-fifth genius of justice. You have now garnered all these stories and all this wisdom. The only thing left to do is step onto the pathway of justice and join the movement for change. I believe in you. I believe you will become the next genius of justice. You have all the tools you need.

Step onto the pathway of justice and keep moving forward. There is no time to waste. The world needs *you* now. I believe you will do the right thing. I am here to walk with you. The geniuses of justice are all here, too. We are excited you have stepped forward to change the world. Let's get moving.

## Reflection to Action Question:

1. How will you use this book and all you have learned about the geniuses of justice to step up and change what you see as wrong in this world?

CPSIA information can be obtained
at www.ICGtesting.com
Printed in the USA
JSHW010301230123
36595JS00002B/13

9 781666 738605